BEYOND GENRE

BEYOND GENRE

Melodrama, Comedy and Romance in Hollywood Films

DEBORAH THOMAS

CAMERON & HOLLIS

A Movie Book

Published by Cameron & Hollis
the publishing imprint of Cameron Books

PO Box 1, Moffat,
Dumfriesshire DG10 9SU, Scotland
Telephone: 01683 220808
Fax: 01683 220012
e-mail: sales@cameronbooks.co.uk
www.cameronbooks.co.uk

First published 2000

British Library Cataloguing-in-Publication Data
A catalogue record for this book is available
from the British Library

ISBN 0-9065506-17-4

Edited by Jill Hollis

Designed by Ian Cameron

Printed and bound in Britain by
MPG Books Ltd, Bodmin

CONTENTS

ACKNOWLEDGEMENTS

This book would not have been possible without the collective support and encouragement of two groups of people who are central to my working life. First of all, I thank my colleagues and friends on the editorial board of *Movie* who, to varying degrees, have aided and abetted this project by reading and commenting upon assorted chapter drafts, as well as by welcoming me into their midst for the past eleven years. Amongst them, I owe particular debts of gratitude to Victor Perkins and Douglas Pye, who have given so much care and valuable time to their responses and whom I thank with affection and respect.

My second collective thank-you goes to my students and former students at the University of Sunderland who have let me try out my ideas on them with exceptional grace and enthusiasm, convincing me that there was something there to be said. Special mention must be made of Elayne Chaplin and Susan Smith, both now lecturers themselves, from whom I continue to learn. On the technical side, I gratefully acknowledge the help and advice of Sue Thompson in the early stages of the book, and of Phil Biggs and Irfan Ul Haq more recently. All three remained calm and cheerful in the face of demands upon them from all directions.

Any merit in this book owes much to the combined editorial efforts of Ian Cameron and Jill Hollis. Though it is difficult to say where the contributions of each of them end and the other's begin, I would like to make particular mention of my indebtedness to Ian's wide-ranging knowledge of American films and his keen eye for design, and to Jill's incisive improvements to the text, offered with such warmth and tact.

More generally, I wish to acknowledge the formative role played by my parents, Rae and Sidney Thomas, and my brother David Thomas, with all of whom I share a love of American films which goes back to childhood and which they did so much to encourage; for this I am grateful and nostalgic in equal measure. My early memories of film-going are intertwined with recollections of particular places and cinemas which they will remember well, from a large converted barn which functioned as a social hall at Meadowbrook Lodge in the Berkshire Hills of western Massachusetts to the far grander spaces of Radio City Music Hall in New York City, and from the Riviera 'art' cinema in Syracuse, New York, to a rather more eccentric local cinema which had better be nameless, run by a couple whose arguments in the back of the auditorium would accompany the films, to the mixed annoyance and amusement of my brother and me. Such richly textured experiences of going to the movies seem to be more and more a thing of the past in the current age of multiplexes, video and DVD.

Finally, but not least, I am grateful beyond words to my daughter Natasha Smith and her father John Smith, each of whom can always make me smile, which is no small thing.

Deborah Thomas
November 2000

CHAPTER ONE

STRUCTURES, MOODS AND WORLDS

Emmy (Diana Lynn): 'You can't tell how a town's gonna take things.'
   The Miracle of Morgan's Creek (Preston Sturges, 1944)

Katie (Ginger Rogers): 'Go someplace where it's safe.'
Anna (Natasha Lytess), her Jewish maid: 'Where?'
      Once upon a Honeymoon (Leo McCarey, 1942)

The intention in this book is to provide an account of mainstream American films in terms of certain broad categories which I shall refer to as the melodramatic, the comedic and the romantic. I would stress at this point that what I'm referring to as the melodramatic and the comedic seem to me to be fundamental, whereas the romantic is less autonomous, as we shall see. Romance seems necessarily to be intertwined with either melodramatic or comedic structures, which is why I shall argue for a mixed terminology for the two romantic hybrids – romantic melodrama and romantic comedy.

My intuition that such issues are important has been provoked both in the classroom and at the movies. In classroom discussions about genre, it quickly becomes apparent that, although there are no problems in identifying particular films as Westerns, horror films, musicals, and so on, or in outlining relevant criteria for these various genres, it is a different matter with terms like melodrama and comedy, which can be both narrowly generic (as in screwball comedy, say, or domestic small-town melodrama) and, at the same time, much broader in ways that cut across the generic field. As well as being aware of the difficulties posed by such terms both for students and for many critics and theorists, I have a powerful sense as an ordinary movie spectator (a sense which I believe is widely shared) that different kinds of viewing experience are available from different kinds of films in ways that go beyond genre. Thus, when I approach films (from a variety of genres) in which it is clear that the main characters will be dogged by an unforgiving fate and that they will almost certainly be caught and punished in some way, I often have to steel myself to watch them. In contrast, my body relaxes when I'm about to look at other films whose tone is very different. What's involved here is an extremely broad anticipation of the kinds of pleasure to be offered or withheld and the kinds of narrative world I'll be invited to inhabit, not in terms of precise settings and events, but in terms of the ways they are experienced by viewers and, to some extent, by the central characters: on one hand, there are narrative worlds that feel repressive and full of danger and, on the other, those that feel more benevolent and safe. Settling down to watch a film is, crucially, a case of getting in the mood for the sort of film one is about to watch.

As seasoned viewers of American films, we experience both a sense of recognition – that is, the feeling that we are in familiar territory and know what to expect – and a simultaneous awareness of the possibility that we may nonetheless be taken by surprise. Such a combination of repetition and difference has often been taken to be a hallmark of film genres in which a formulaic framework gives rise to a large number of variations. Thus, Douglas Pye suggests that 'The recognition of works as belonging to a specific genre may be seen as the result of . . . the intersection of a range of categories, the interplay of which generates meaning within a context narrow enough for recognition of the genre to take place but wide enough to allow enormous individual variation' ('Genre and Movies' in *Movie* 20, Spring 1975, p.32). One of the merits of Pye's account is that it warns against seeing genres 'as essentially *definable* and therefore [. . .] genre criticism as in need of defining criteria. This is to imagine genre as a kind of Platonic form, having an independent existence . . .' (p.30). Instead, he speaks of 'broad tendencies of narrative' (p.33) in combination with 'local conditions of various kinds', such as typical recurring plots and settings, structural oppositions, conventional character types, iconography and themes.

There is a close affinity between my own approach and Pye's claim that 'we may find common tendencies across a number of genres we commonly think of as distinct. Generic differences emerge from the combination of these basic tendencies and the more local conventions.' Thus, a given genre is made up of a range of inflections (through local conventions) of broader narrative modes. However, whereas much work has been done on the nature of such local conventions (the generically specific aspects of various genres), we remain at a much more preliminary stage in thinking about what might consititute broader tendencies across genres. Pye's account offers as possible candidates Northrop Frye's five fictional modes, 'defined in terms of the range and power of action of the protagonist' (p.32) and also Frye's 'further distinction . . . between tragedy and comedy' (p.33) conceived in terms of whether the hero is isolated from society or integrated within it. Although there is some connection between these categories and my own (particularly insofar as comedy is a central term in both), I shall be stepping aside from the particularities of Frye's various modes and distinctions, Pye himself finding them 'unsatisfactory as final categories'. I shall, however, be taking up the challenge of Pye's article as a whole.

In contrast to the clarity of Douglas Pye's account, there is throughout the critical writing on melodrama, comedy and romance considerable slippage between the views of them as genres and as categories of a broader type. One of the problems in construing them as genres is precisely the fact that many of the most central characteristics attributed to them appear to apply to films of many genres, making their generic identities dissolve in our grasp. It may be said that, in such instances, the distinction between 'local conditions' and 'broad tendencies' largely breaks down, which is not the case with, say, the Western, (the central focus of Pye's concern). Most obviously, in the case of romance, the presence of mutual heterosexual desire as a central concern is far from limited to films of a single genre (though admittedly romance is rarely put forward as a genre, presumably because it is so pervasive). Richard Maltby and Ian Craven (in *Hollywood Cinema: An Introduction*, Blackwell, 1995, pp.132-133) attempt to correct what for them is an oversight by adding romance to standard lists of genres: 'In the generic mapping of Hollywood, the quantitatively overwhelming omission is that of romance, which features as the principal or secondary plot in 90 per cent of Hollywood's output.' However, it seems to me that such pervasiveness is precisely a reason not to see romance as a genre. Steve Neale and Frank Krutnik refer to Brian Henderson's view on the matter, which asserts not only that one should avoid construing romance as a genre, but that even romantic comedy is far too broad a category to be construed in that way: 'Because of the prevalence of elements of romance and comedy in the majority of Hollywood films, Brian Henderson raises doubts about the viability of isolating the romantic comedy as a distinct film category' (in Neale and Krutnik's *Popular Film and Television Comedy*, Routledge, 1990, p.137).

This problem of generic specificity versus a more wide-ranging category of some sort is also widely acknowledged in studies of melodrama and comedy. Thus, Christine Gledhill, in her introduction to *Home Is Where The Heart Is* (BFI, 1987), says, 'A central problem is melodrama's status not just as a cinematic genre, but as a mode with formative roots in the nineteenth century' (p.1). In this latter sense, it is 'a pervasive mode across popular culture . . . It refers not only to a type of aesthetic practice but also to a way of viewing the world'. Andrew Horton makes a comparable claim that '. . . comedy has been viewed in recent years as a particular *quality* . . . or vision' (in Horton, ed., *Comedy/Cinema/Theory*, University of California Press, 1991, p.3). Gerald Mast (in *The Comic Mind: Comedy and the Movies*, New English Library, 1973, p.11, footnote) speaks in a similar way of the comic climate that 'persists throughout a comic film'.

Characterising the precise nature of the relationship between the general and particular uses of each term is difficult. Neale and Krutnik acknowledge that 'Perhaps the most striking thing about comedy is the immense variety and range of its forms' (Neale and Krutnik, p.10), construing this formal diversity as subsumed under the rubric of a single genre. In some ways, however, their assertion that there exists within the comedy genre a variety of forms may be comparable to Gledhill's identification of a variety of melodramatic genres – 'Melodrama was at best a fragmented generic category' (Gledhill, p.6) – within the melodramatic mode. The difficulty of knowing how to interpret such terms as 'genre' and 'mode' presents itself throughout writings on melodrama, comedy and romance, for example, in André Bazin's statement that 'Comedy was in reality the most serious genre in Hollywood, in the sense that it reflected, through the comic mode, the deepest moral and social beliefs of American life' (quoted in Horton, p.3).

I want to argue that to take as genres the very broad categories that I'm calling melodramatic and comedic (along with their romantic hybrids) is to make what Gilbert Ryle calls a 'category mistake'. In *The Concept of Mind* (Penguin, 1990, first published 1949), Ryle gives two particularly relevant examples of what he means.

> A foreigner visiting Oxford or Cambridge for the first time is shown a number of colleges, libraries, playing fields, museums, scientific departments and administrative offices. He then asks 'But where is the University? [. . .]' It has then to be explained to him that the University is not another collateral institution, some ulterior counterpart to the colleges, laboratories and offices which he has seen. The University is just the way in which all that he has already seen is organized [. . .] His mistake lay in his innocent assumption that it was correct to speak of Christ Church, the Bodleian Library, the Ashmolean Museum *and* the

> University, to speak, that is, as if 'the University' stood for an extra
> member of the class of which these other units are members. (pp.17-18)

> A foreigner watching his first game of cricket learns what are the functions
> of the bowlers, the batsmen, the fielders, the umpires and the scorers.
> He then says 'But there is no one left on the field to contribute the famous
> element of team-spirit. I see who does the bowling, the batting and the
> wicket-keeping; but I do not see whose role it is to exercise *esprit de corps*.'
> Once more, it would have to be explained that he was looking for the
> wrong type of thing. Team-spirit is not another cricketing operation
> supplementary to all of the other special tasks. It is, roughly, the
> keenness with which each of the special tasks is performed, and
> performing a task keenly is not performing two tasks. (p.18)

Ryle gives other examples too, but I've concentrated on those which seem most relevant to my own concerns. I find it helpful to view the melodramatic and the comedic as, on one hand, distinctive structures (like Ryle's 'University'), and, on the other, as distinctive ways of being a genre film (having something of the force of Ryle's 'keenly': thus, performing a task keenly is something like being a Western melodramatically or comedically, though it remains no less a Western, in terms of its specific genre, in either case). My ambition in this book is to uncover exactly what such structures and ways of being entail. Part of the problem is finding a vocabulary which will clarify rather than confuse. The terms 'melodramatic' and 'comedic' are potential sources of bewilderment, given the histories of usage which they trail behind them. In deploying these terms, I am indicating an intention to link my use of them with the sense in which they are already used – or, at least, with some of the films to which these terms have been taken to refer – but I also wish to offer a new definition of them which both broadens and constricts their application. For example, not all films generally thought of as comedies will prove to be comedic in my sense of the term, and films not generally thought to be melodramas may turn out, in my terms, to be melodramatic after all: it is probably accurate to say that overall my understanding of the melodramatic and the comedic will tend to expand the domain of the former while contracting that of the latter.

I have already given some indication of the contrasting moods which the melodramatic and the comedic evoke for the viewers of such films and the bodily states which are adopted in response: on one hand, a sense of being invited into a place of danger and entrapment and a defensive tightening or hardening of our bodies, on the other, a sense of safety and a corresponding bodily relaxation. One might expect our feelings as viewers to be mirrored by those of the central characters in the films – after all, they already inhabit the narrative worlds we're being invited to enter – but such congruence between us and them is far from certain and, in any case, is far more likely with regard to melodramatic than to comedic films. As I'll argue in Chapter Three, the world of comedy appears to be safe partly because we perceive it as a fictional world with a benevolent director pulling the strings. In contrast, the oppressiveness of the melodramatic world seems to be inherent in its social fabric and conditions rather than originating in a malevolent figure outside. For characters in comedic films to know that they are safe, they would need to be aware that they are characters in a comedic film, whereas melodramatic characters can feel the weight of their oppression without the same degree of self-consciousness.

Of course, melodramatic characters may mistakenly believe themselves to be free from oppressive determinants, unaware of the malign fate closing in on them as well as of its institutional and ideological underpinnings. Indeed, such blindness has some-times been taken to be a central characteristic of the melodramatic protagonist. Similarly, comedic characters may mistakenly believe themselves to be persecuted and entrapped (rather than set free for better things), their demeanours often increasingly frantic and frustrated (consider Cary Grant's character, David Huxley, for example, in the 1938 Howard Hawks comedy, *Bringing Up Baby*). Nevertheless, melodramatic characters are far more likely than comedic characters to experience the mood or 'feel' of their narrative world in ways that match viewers' experiences of it: comedic characters would have to be aware that they inhabit a fictional world. From the point of view of the characters, a comedic film's resolution is therefore more precarious than the resolution of a melodramatic film, coming as it seems to do without guarantees (that is, there is no way of their knowing whether its happy circumstances will last), in contrast to the finality with which melodramatic characters may feel themselves to be sinking beneath the burden of their fates. Whereas being safe or in danger is, in the first instance, a condition of the characters, and only vi-cariously ours, an accurate awareness of the conditions of a film's narrative world and, in consequence, the eliciting of an appropriate emotional response to the broader picture belongs mainly to us, especially with respect to comedic films.

I am also suggesting that the melodramatic and the comedic are alternative struc-tures, and some introductory words must be offered in explanation of the structural aspects of these categories. My argument is that the melodramatic and the comedic provide contrasting ways of structuring the space of the narrative world. For example, melodramatic films typically contrast a social space of some sort (a domestic setting, a small town, a community, or some other, more general representation of civilisation) with an alternative space (the city's criminal underworld, a battlefield, the wilderness, for example) where social values and expectations to some extent break down. Both sorts of space give rise to their own characteristic fantasies. Thus, inherent in the nor-mal social space, where men and women settle down together in marriage and dom-esticity, are corresponding male and female versions of fantasies which emphasise the struggles for dominance between men and women in what is a rigidly hierarchical world. These may take the form of wishful fantasies of power or, as their flip-side, anxious fantasies of disempowerment, though in the context of domestic small-town melodramas, the fantasies may be about no more than the appearance of power, using metaphors around physical augmentation and diminishment – as in *The Incredible Shrinking Man* (Jack Arnold, 1956) or *Bigger than Life* (Nicholas Ray, 1956) – to express the desire to save face or the fear of losing face, particularly for the domesticated male. In contrast, the space of adventure away from the everyday social world embodies a fantasy of masculine escape where male toughness replaces augmentation: that is, fantasies of violent self-assertion replace those which offer a mere appearance of domination – a front for the benefit of the outside world – within the marital and familial home.

13

Of course, many melodramatic films lack onscreen representations of one or other of these two spaces, but both remain implicit points of reference for the melodramatic, and their relationship constitutes its characteristic structure. Thus, for melodramatic films set wholly within the space of violent male adventure away from the normal social world, some sense of 'home' or 'community' (whether as a dream of unattainable domestic or familial bliss or as a trap to be avoided at all costs) is often implied. Similarly, characters in domestic melodramas set wholly within the home and/or small town may long for an escape to an alternative and more exciting place, which never materialises in the onscreen narrative world but is nonetheless of considerable motive and imaginative force (Frank Capra's *It's a Wonderful Life*, 1946, is the quintessential example of this, but there are many more).

Within this basic melodramatic structure, romance can appear either as a relationship under siege from the repressive world outside, the space of the romantic couple tightly circumscribed in defensive withdrawal from their surroundings, or as a battleground where the couple engage in a struggle for dominance. The longing for something better, in this context, can only be a pipe-dream: one might think of the lovers in *West Side Story* (Robert Wise/Jerome Robbins, 1961) who sing of 'a place somewhere' as they try to imagine themselves outside a world that has precisely no place for their romance, or of Beth (Gloria Henry) in Fritz Lang's *Rancho Notorious* (1952) talking to her fiancé, Vern (Arthur Kennedy), about their eventual life together at the aptly named Lost Cloud Ranch (at this point, no more than an insubstantial dream for the future) only moments before she is brutally raped and murdered, and Vern is set on a course of self-destructive revenge. In both cases, the impossibility of the idealised romance is seen in terms of the lack of a place to shelter within the inhospitable spaces of the melodramatic narrative world.

It is a central aspect of comedic films, by contrast, that the social space within them is transformable into something better than the repressive, hierarchical world of melodramatic films, so that fantasies of transformation within this space replace fantasies of escape to a space elsewhere. The romantic couple can aspire to a state of mutuality and playful improvisation, and, rather than ending up embattled or under siege, may find a benevolent and sheltering community to welcome them in its midst. In melodramatic films, the various spaces – the social space, the male space of violent adventure, the space of the romantic couple locked in battle or under siege – tend to be rigidly self-contained and set against one another, while in comedic films, the transformed communal space is more fluid with the romantic couple more integrated within it – a place of permeable boundaries and passage through them. However, it is important to note that many films are neither wholly one thing nor another: for example, the romantic space of the couple may both contract away from and expand into the surrounding community in the course of a single film, as the film moves between the melodramatic and the comedic – an extremely common phenomenon. A film's generic identity, on the other hand, tends to be more stable: a Western generally remains a Western all the way through.

What I have been indicating so far are the 'feels' of melodramatic and comedic films and their characteristic ways of structuring the space within them. I have also suggested a link between their respective spatial configurations and moods, and, for example, certain recurring fantasies centred around power (in melodramatic films) and a sort of transformative and liberating mutuality (in comedic ones). By 'fantasies', I mean particular ways of imagining any of a number of common concerns which occur across the full range of American films – concerns about the nature of society and the individual's relation to it, concerns about love and how to sustain it, and so on. I have in mind something like Michael Wood's description, in *America in the Movies* (Secker & Warburg, 1975), of worries 'that nag at us from the edges of consciousness . . . without forcing us to look at them too closely' (pp.16-17). Films, for Wood, represent not so much a flight from our problems as 'a rearrangement of our problems into shapes which tame them, which disperse them to the margins of our attention' (p.18). I prefer to talk about concerns, rather than worries, since some of them may provoke eager interest rather than anxiety. Nevertheless, it is clear that we are talking about the same sort of thing, even if what he calls 'the shapes which tame them' are rewritten, in my account, in terms of specifically melodramatic and comedic fantasies, or ways of imagining, such concerns. In this sense, all American films are fantasies, though they are not fantasy films in the much narrower sense of films in which the narrative includes supernatural events or events the explanation of which 'hesitates', as Tzvetan Todorov puts it, between natural and supernatural paradigms (in *The Fantastic: A Structural Approach to a Literary Genre*, Cornell University Press, 1975).

Before proceeding, it may be useful to ask whether what I've been calling the melodramatic, the comedic and the romantic constitute necessary and sufficient categories to cover all possible narrative worlds generated by mainstream American films since the introduction of sound (I shall not be considering examples from outside this domain). I have argued against using fantasy as part of an alternative schema, both because, in my opinion, the term can be applied to all mainstream American films, and because, in other people's use of it to designate films about the supernatural, it seems to me to be narrowly generic, rather than an example of the broad – but not all-inclusive – sort of category across genres which I'm after. Are there any other categories that would do as well or better? Christine Gledhill, for example, sees melodrama as a mode 'rivalling realism in its claim to found the popular cinema' (Gledhill, p.1). What about a schema based on these two terms?

The main problem in contrasting realism with melodrama quickly becomes evident when we try to decide which films go into which category. Presumably, the attraction of both realism and melodrama as founding modes derives from the fact that the roots of the popular American cinema can be seen to lie in both. That is, the popular American cinema has a dual origin (at least), and many of its products – rather than being divided into two sub-categories, some realist, some melodramatic – are simultaneously both (though the realism/melodrama schema makes no room for the comedic, a serious drawback for any schema which aspires to comprehensiveness). Realism is such a fraught and ambiguous term – sometimes designating a style, for example, sometimes a representation of a particular sort of social world – that I will leave it to one side in the discussion that follows, except in a very limited sense. Raymond Williams's point, as presented by Terry Lovell (in *Pictures of Reality: Aesthetics, Politics and Pleasure*, BFI, 1980, p.65), is that all realisms have in common the claim 'that the business of art is first and foremost "to show things as they really are" ', despite differences amongst various realisms as to how such a reality is to be understood. I accept that the great majority of mainstream American films are realist insofar as the physical world that they present is intended to 'show things as they really are' in two ways: first, in terms of a set of common reference points – that is, people, places and events which are either narrowly historical (Abraham Lincoln, Palm Beach, the Cold War, say) or more broadly cultural (suburbia, for example, as a recognisable cultural location); second, in terms of a shared understanding of what is possible or impossible in such a place (its laws of nature). Even where the scientific laws which are normally taken to govern our world no longer hold – as in supernatural horror films, say, or fantasies involving ghosts or guardian angels – there is generally also a sense of resistance within the narrative world: its rules are being broken as well, and such transgressions are often met with scepticism on the part of characters within the film (as when, George Bailey/James Stewart in *It's a Wonderful Life*, is confronted with his guardian angel).

I am not claiming that such worlds, or the specific locations within them which are highlighted by particular films, are continuous with ours – clearly, as fictions, they exist on another level altogether – rather that their continuity with our world is part of the fiction and underlies the possibility of continuities across films of different genres, even if, in some cases, the possibilities seem much more blocked and difficult to conceive. Thus, there are numerous examples of returning soldiers in war films who (by a change in geographical position from 'overseas' to 'back home') step into the world of domestic melodrama without any contradiction. Similarly, given a sufficient passage of time, it is at least plausible that a Western hero (or his descendants) might return from the wilderness to find civilisation transformed into the post-industrial and alienating urban space of *film noir*. I am not saying that all of these journeys actually take place – though some do – but rather that the underlying assumption behind mainstream American films is that they refer to the same connected narrative world, even if their versions of it vary both spatially and temporally.

The difficulty in imagining spatial continuities across films of different genres lies not so much in their having different preferred locations (or, in some having more flexibility of location than others), but in the fact that there are frequently generically specific ways of representing, and thus constituting, such locations which appropriate them for a specific genre. Although *film noir* tends to be set in the city, it is a very different city from that of sophisticated comedies of remarriage, say, because of its generically determined mode of representation. Do these genre-specific ways of representing spatial locations lead to fundamental incompatibilities between genres which hopelessly fragment the narrative world across the generic field, or do they simply lead to productive tensions comparable to those within a single given genre (like, for example, the tension between the small town and the city in *film noir*, or that between civilisation and the wilderness in the Western)?

The implied continuity of the narrative world which is taken to extend beyond the framed portions of it which we are permitted to see in a given film or genre may support extreme generic shifts or conflicts within individual films as well as between them. Even a shift as extreme as that between melodrama and comedy can be accommodated within a single film, as some critics have pointed out (though they have usually done so at the level of specific melodramatic and comic genres). My own emphasis will be on the shifting structures, which I've been calling melodramatic and comedic in a broader sense, whose interactions within films of all genres seem so pervasive. In the chapters which follow, I shall present close analyses of a number of films of various genres which suggest what such interactions might involve and exactly what is at stake when the melodramatic and the comedic come into conflict.

In the matter of vocabulary, and in the interests of clarity, I have preferred, wherever possible, to avoid using 'melodrama', 'comedy' and 'romance' as the names of particular genres, reserving them (usually in their adjectival forms: 'melodramatic', 'comedic', 'romantic') as the names of broad categories which cut across generic boundaries and exist at a different level altogether. It seems most helpful to see genres as much narrower categories of film, amongst which I would want to include specific melodramatic and comic genres as they have been variously set forth in the critical literature. There is, however, no agreed terminology here, rather, a number of overlapping terms such as domestic or small-town melodrama, the woman's film, screwball comedy, the comedy of remarriage, domestic comedy, and so on. It is clear from the recurrence of the general terms as part of the names of more specific genres (domestic *melodrama*, screwball *comedy*, and so forth) that these groups of films are commonly understood to be subgenres which are structurally subordinate to broader categories or genres, but these are not the same sort of thing as those broad categories I've been proposing as fundamental. Though I would prefer to avoid the confusions which will inevitably follow from the juxtaposition of this usage with my own, I am certainly not hostile to the possibility of a relationship between subgenres and genres which links under a common rubric domestic melodrama and the woman's film, say, but still distinguishes them both from Westerns, musicals and other less intimately related genres, though, of course, films from any of these categories may be melodramatic in my sense.

The relationship between genres and my proposed melodramatic, comedic or romantic categories is not comparable to that between subgenres and genres, where all films belonging to a subgenre necessarily belong to the corresponding genre (all vampire films, for example, necessarily belonging to the horror genre). I wish to allow for the possibility that some horror films, say, may be melodramatic, while others are comedic. Despite the potentially confusing overlap of terminology where melodrama and comedy are concerned, I would even want to allow for cases where a musical comedy, for example, could most profitably be seen in terms of melodramatic structures, and a domestic melodrama in terms of comedic ones. Such cases may be rare or non-existent, but, despite their implausibility, they are at least logically possible insofar as the broadly melodramatic and comedic are different in essence from our understanding of specifically melodramatic and comic genres. Thus, Robin Wood suggests that domestic comedy 'is built on the entrapment of the male' ('The American Family Comedy: from *Meet Me In St. Louis* to *The Texas Chainsaw Massacre*' in *Wide Angle* vol. 3, no. 2, 1979, p.8), and it is certainly feasible to see a film like Vincente Minnelli's *Father of the Bride* (1950) – one of Wood's examples of domestic comedy – as broadly melodramatic in my terms.

I must admit that I am at more of a loss to come up with an example that goes the other way: that is, a film belonging to a specifically melodramatic genre which, in my terms, is broadly comedic. It seems to be a *sine qua non* of the definitions of all comic genres that they include an intention to make us laugh, and I have been using the term 'comic' to designate this, rather than 'comedic.' I shall be suggesting that the essence of the comedic, in contrast, is a particular sort of transformation of the narrative world whose details will be explored later on, which may or may not elicit laughter as the primary response. Thus, films other than comedies (a Western like Howard Hawks's *Rio Bravo*, 1959, say) may provide examples of the comedic, rather than the melodramatic, even if our pleasures don't issue in laughter. If laughter is not a necessary defining trait of the comedic, neither is it sufficient, since we may be encouraged to laugh at those caught up in repressive melodramatic fantasies as well as in comedic ones, as in the case of *Father of the Bride*, as we've already seen, where, to reiterate Robin Wood's claim, the world of Stanley Banks (Spencer Tracy) is 'built on [his] entrapment'. In contrast, what the various melodramatic genres have been claimed to have in common is more complex than a mere propensity to elicit a fixed reaction equivalent (and perhaps opposite) to laughter. So each comic genre represents the locations, characters and events in its designated films in a particular way – as funny – even if they have not been transformed through comedic fantasy: even if it is our own repressively hierarchical world that is funny. At their most un-comedic extreme, comic genres include films of so-called 'black humour' such as Alfred Hitchcock's *Psycho* (1960), in which what is funny and what is repressive most outrageously merge, producing laughter that is extremely uncomfortable and hollow.

Across the various genres traditionally grouped together under the label of melo-drama, there is significantly less range, partly because their unifying features are much more complex, requiring a far greater number of elements in common: aesthetic, the-matic, emotional, and narrative criteria all play a part. But, because different accounts privilege different aspects, it is hard to pin down what all melodramatic genres have in common (and do not share with genres like the Western or *film noir*, for example) which constitutes their peculiarly melodramatic aspect at the level of genre. Until we know what such an ingredient might be, it is impossible to determine the extent to which such genres *as genres* overlap with or depart from broader melodramatic structures and dynamics. It seems to me that, until a proper taxonomy of the various melodramatic genres has been produced, all we can say is that we can make no easy assumptions on the basis of genre alone. The detailed workings of individual films must be our primary evidence, bypassing considerations of genre, at least in the present account.

A preoccupation of much writing on melodrama and comedy (and their romantic variants) is the nature of the relationship between them, though this is usually dis-cussed in terms of specific melodramatic or comic genres. Thus, Robin Wood discusses 'the opposition of two Hollywood genres . . . the Domestic Comedy and the Domestic Melodrama (or "Woman's Picture").' As previously mentioned, he argues 'that the former is built on the entrapment of the male, the latter on that of the female' (Wood, 1979, p.8). Wes D. Gehring is interested in the fact that 'screwball comedy is a genre of indeterminate time and space, like the musical and the melodrama' (*Screwball Comedy: A Genre of Madcap Romance*, Greenwood Press, 1986, p.156), and Kathleen Rowe is even more insistent than Gehring on fundamental links between melodrama and comedy: 'Romantic comedy exists in the same kind of generic tension with melodrama that Frye finds between comedy and tragedy . . . [and] usually contains a potential melodrama, and melodrama . . . contains a potential romantic comedy' ('Comedy, Melodrama and Gender' in Kristine Brunovska Karnick and Henry Jenkins (eds), *Classical Hollywood Comedy*, Routledge, 1995, p.49).

Neale and Krutnik, too, point out that 'comedy can come surprisingly close, in its concerns as well as in many of its structural features, to the genre we tend now to think of as melodrama' (Neale and Krutnik, p.13). They cite *Bachelor Mother* (Garson Kanin, 1939) as an example of a film which, though they designate it as a romantic comedy, 'flirts with and disavows the emotional problematic familiar from the "unwed mother" melodrama' (p.158), though I would like to modify and extend what they say somewhat. The film is about a woman who finds an abandoned baby which no one will believe is not hers. Neale and Krutnik's question is, 'We *know* that Polly is *not* the child's mother, but *what if* she were?' So their suggestion is that within this comedy there lurks a potential melodrama. But it is also true that a potential melodrama is lurking in another sense, since the presence of the actual mother of the abandoned baby is implied elsewhere in the film's narrative world, though in the part of it which remains offscreen, and, perhaps, in the past (that is, she may be dead). In other words, one of the assumptions embedded in the film's world is that the baby must have had a mother: though she's absent from the film itself, she is implied within the larger world generated by the narrative. A shift in point of view from the heroine to the mother would have pushed the film towards melodrama rather than towards comedy. A relatively minor character in a film may carry the potential for such a shift, and the film's apparent uniformity may depend on edging such a character from that part of the narrative world represented onscreen. A good example of such an attempt is the exclusion of Potter (Lionel Barrymore) from the celebration of community in the final scene of *It's a Wonderful Life* (though the film as a whole – and even that scene, despite Potter's exclusion – retains melodramatic elements). Another is the exclusion (through his death) of Harry Beaton (Hugh Laing) from the idealised community of Vincente Minnelli's *Brigadoon* (1954), an example to which I shall return in more detail shortly, and again at the end of Chapter Four. Point of view is clearly crucial to our sense of a movie's world. The extent of our access to the various spaces of the narrative world, but also the extent to which we are given access to particular characters as they move within and across such spaces, are crucial factors in determining our sense of the sort of experience we're being invited to share in a given film.

The issue of point of view is an enormously complex and demanding one whose ramifications can hardly be accommodated here. In one sense, point of view comprises everything a film does to create its stance or viewpoint with regard to its narrative world, and not purely in visual terms: thus, it includes, for example, epistemological and ideological aspects, as well as ways of seeing from a particular orientation or set of orientations in space and time. A central plank of my argument throughout this book is that a film's melodramatic or comedic nature (or a romantic version of either) is an important component of its overall point of view, just as its point of view is partly constitutive of whether it is melodramatic or comedic, or a shifting configuration involving both. But that is not precisely what I wish to focus on now. Rather, I wish to pursue a bit further the idea that such shifts may be a consequence of changes in our orientation in a more specific and localised sense: as well as positioning ourselves in line with the point of view of the film as a whole, we may also imaginatively align ourselves with characters who are marginal to the film's project or less in tune with its position overall, provided that they 'speak' to us in some way.

Put more simply, a film's point of view is clearly not reducible to that of the characters – or even a privileged character – within it, but includes an attitude or orientation towards the various characters (whether one of ironic detachment, sympathetic involvement, moral condemnation, or whatever) as well as some sort of epistemological relationship which is never precisely one of identity (where we see and know precisely what they do, nothing more nor less), and a spatial positioning which is not identical with theirs. Seeing how a film's narrative events and resolutions feel from the point of view of a character who is not centrally located within the spatial, narrative and ideological structures of a film (for example, a character who is often offscreen, say, or whose desires are not a central motivating thrust in what happens) may provide insight into the extent to which a film's melodramatic or comedic atmosphere is dependent upon the minimising of troubling countercurrents to its resolutions in these terms. In contrast, where a film treats such characters sympathetically, perhaps, in some cases, to an even greater extent than it treats its ostensible hero or heroine, the resultant mixture of the melodramatic, the comedic and the romantic (if it exists) may be an intended or openly constitutive aspect of its overall point of view, producing a complexity which enriches the film rather than pushing it to incoherence.

Though not all divided points of view are examples of such conflict, I shall concentrate on those that are. For instance, a character in a comedic film may not be susceptible to its fantasies or, in any way, transformed by them for the better; or a character in a melodramatic narrative world may seemingly escape (if this is possible) its particular economies of power and displaced desire; or, alternatively, in what I suspect occurs most frequently, a romantic narrative may deny to some of its less central characters the satisfactions – or even the possibilities – of mutual erotic desire. That this happens in romantic films is so obvious as to be commonplace, though it is certainly not inevitable: we shall see, in Chapter Four, how Tom Corbett's 'romance' with his son (and, eventually, with Elizabeth/Shirley Jones), in *The Courtship of Eddie's Father* (Vincente Minnelli, 1963), opens up a larger shared space which incorporates the relationship of Dollye (Stella Stevens) with Norm (Jerry Van Dyke), or, in Chapter Three, how Snoodles (Rudy Vallee) and Maude (Mary Astor) are provided with romantic partners when Gerry (Claudette Colbert) and Tom Jeffers (Joel McCrea) are reconciled at the end of *The Palm Beach Story* (Preston Sturges, 1942). More unusual is the film that includes in its overall point of view an explicit awareness and acknowledgment of such an exclusion of a secondary (though nonetheless sympathetic and deserving) character from its ostensible fantasy of reciprocated desire.

This is what seems to me to be happening in Hitchcock's *To Catch a Thief* (1955), an intriguing example of a film whose complexity increases once we recognise and acknowledge not just the points of view of its central romantic figures, John Robie (Cary Grant) and Francie Stevens (Grace Kelly), but also that of a particular secondary character, Francie's mother, Mrs Stevens (Jessie Royce Landis). Not only is Jessie Stevens the one who notices Robie first ('Mmm. Handsome. I wouldn't mind buying *that* for you'), but she and Robie strike up an instant rapport when he drops a 10,000-franc token down the bosom of a woman at the gambling casino, and their gazes meet across the table as they share the joke. Robie's merriment seems genuine, as well as his appreciation of Mrs Stevens, and the two continue to find they have much in common, as Jessie's thoughts of her late husband – and her present loneliness without him – rise readily to the surface. However, her thoughts about missing her husband and wanting to put Robie in his place must be suppressed and can only be permitted to emerge vicariously through pairing off Robie and her daughter, a reading confirmed by her later remark, 'If I were Francie's age, you'd sound too good to be true.' As a younger version of her mother (earlier that day Francie has remarked, 'There's not much difference between us'), Francie, like her necklace, is an imitation, presenting no more than an impossibly beautiful and flawless surface, while her mother, whose jewels are genuine, is, in some sense, the real thing. Francie's anger when her mother's jewels are stolen during the night of the fireworks display and her assumption that Robie is guilty, as well as her mother's growing alliance with him by that point (Francie sends for the police and Jessie helps him to get away) provide further support for this reading of the film's central romantic relationship as a screen for a more marginal one which can reveal itself only indirectly.

Thus, Hitchcock's film is an example of a more general tendency whereby films which give us access to and sympathetic involvement with the points of view of characters whose desires are not central motivating factors in their narrative resolutions may disturb such resolutions or render them ambiguous, particularly in terms of the playing out of romantic fantasies. So-called happy endings, in particular, are rarely happy for everyone, especially where romance is concerned. Hitchcock's merit lies in allowing Robie to resist (to some extent) Francie's beauty and to direct his smiles elsewhere, while at the same time giving Jessie's desires a voice, however wishful and resigned. His films make explicit what is more commonly implicit: the way that mainstream fantasies often swamp more marginal points of view and determine whether a film is predominantly melodramatic, comedic or romantic, and the shape its resolution will take.

Thus far, I have been presenting a case for seeing the melodramatic, the comedic and their romantic hybrids as the fundamental categories of American films. While melodramatic fantasies respond to a hierarchical social setting whose privileges are heavily dependent upon markers of difference based on such things as gender, class and race, comedic fantasies use cinematic 'magic' to transform the world into something more spontaneous and, at the same time, safe, providing a home (as opposed to a battleground) for reciprocal erotic desire. However, another, equally important, strand to my argument is that the boundaries between the melodramatic and the comedic are by no means fixed.

Comedic films seem to have to strive continually to keep melodrama at bay. The melodramatic is revealed within them sometimes through the merest suggestion of an oppressive world offscreen, sometimes more forcefully as an intrusion at the edges of the frame or narrative, and sometimes as such an invasive presence that the film's comedic space is reduced to a very small community within a much larger melodramatic world. Melodramatic characters may be present in the form of villains or frustrated lovers who must be killed off or ejected from the comedic space within the narrative world if its comedic climate is to be preserved, though such ejections also function as reminders of the larger, less benevolent world outside and may thus continue to trouble the viewer's confidence in the possibilities of the comedic fully escaping its dominion. Finally, the same space or character may shift from melodramatic to

21

comedic in the course of a film. There is a certain lack of symmetry here in that, while comedy at its most complex seems to 'know' the melodramatic world outside, melodrama does not seem to recognise the comedic in any corresponding way: this very blindness to alternatives, and the sense of narrative dead ends which it embodies, are part of its pessimism and repressive atmosphere. The reason for this is fairly clear if one accepts the assumption that the world in which we live and in which movies are made has a kinship with the melodramatic – in being hierarchical, gendered, class-based and so on – rather than with the comedic. This is the necessary starting point for *all* films of whatever type – the context, that is, in which they take on meaning – and, whereas comedy can, to varying degrees, either accept or turn its back on this recognition, melodrama, by its more intimate mirroring of this world and the fantasies it generates, is unable to do so, nor can it, in good faith, attribute anything approaching a comedic quality to the world outside its borders, since there is none to be found.

Romance is the fantasy common to both the melodramatic and the comedic, appearing in hybrid form as either romantic melodrama or romantic comedy. But whereas the fantasy of mutual erotic desire finds a welcoming home within the latter, it finds itself embattled and fundamentally at odds with the requirements of the former: the romantic couple is under siege both from the outside and, to the extent that the couple have internalised its values and its commitment to gendered roles and differences in status and power, from within. Comedic films, too, as we've seen, may include a degree of conflict with a surrounding or impinging melodramatic world outside, though the romantic couple, where it exists, is typically located within a sheltering community which acts as a buffer between the lovers and the harsh realities of any more unsympathetic and more hierarchical setting. For example, we shall see how, films like *To Be or Not to Be* (Ernst Lubitsch, 1942) or *Brigadoon* or *The Courtship of Eddie's Father*, a melodramatic world pushes inward on the couple or small community, while, at the same time, more comedic values strive to express themselves in opposition to the melodramatic world outside. Thus, the troupe of actors in *To Be or Not to Be* opens up a safe passage out of the unyielding Nazi world of occupied Warsaw by embracing such values as improvisation, communal endeavour and a greater tolerance of female freedom within marriage, while the 'feminised' and 'musicalised' village of Brigadoon is made possible by its refusal of all contact with the much more repressive world of modern-day New York City. Brigadoon has nothing to offer the embittered and frustrated Harry Beaton who, in turn, is a threat to Brigadoon's existence until he is himself destroyed by Jeff (Van Johnson), his counterpart from New York. In both these films, the comedic world is able to come up with a localised alternative to the melodramatic world which does not so much involve a defeat of that world as an escape from its jurisdiction to a physically separate place (Great Britain and Brigadoon respectively, instead of occupied Poland and New York), though the melodramatic world continues to exist in a place apart. In *The Courtship of Eddie's Father*, as we'll see, the outcome is more open, and the melodramatic and comedic spaces are more intimately linked, but the same sense of tension between them remains.

Of course, the symbolic spaces of melodramatic films are far from gender-neutral. Thus, although the space of the social world (whether construed as civilisation in general or the more private space of the marital home) is where men and women come together – most intimately in the romantic space embedded within it – the fantasised 'elsewhere' of melodrama is a male domain. In melodramas where a male character's desire for a particular woman entails domesticity as its consequence, he may take flight from the everyday social world and assert his freedom from such entanglements through displaced shows of violence against various foes. Such scenarios, as we'll see in *The Searchers* (John Ford, 1956) and *Schindler's List* (Steven Spielberg, 1993), unsurprisingly tend to be centred on men, and they constitute the vast majority of melodramatic films.

Romantic melodramas, on the other hand, or domestic melodramas implying a past romance which has already locked the central male character into the domestic space through marriage, are more likely to generate fantasies of augmentation and diminishment (rather than fantasies of toughness) which have complementary male and female versions, either of which may dominate in a given film, though its complementary opposite is always (at least covertly) implied. So, although I shall concentrate upon male fantasies and points of view in the melodramatic films selected, it would require only a slight imaginative shift in our orientation within those melodramas set within the everyday social space to conjure up alternative scenarios giving more prominence to corresponding female fantasies. It is important to remember, however, that, in the case of some films where we're not given enough to go on (in *The Incredible Shrinking Man*, say, as opposed to *Bigger than Life*), these are scenarios that might have been, rather than those that are actually present in some form, however implicit or attenuated, within the films.

Similarly, in the case of the comedic, although strategies of comedic regression and male heroics are orientated towards transformations of their male characters, romantic comedy, by its nature as a fantasy of mutuality, may involve transformations of both women and men. Although we won't be looking at all possible comedic strategies, the fantasies I shall examine will show that some version of romance – whether active or dormant, fresh or stale – seems important in making a female point of view accessible, and this appears to apply to both melodramatic and comedic films. In the case of maternal melodramas – as is also the case with Tom Corbett and his son in *The Courtship of Eddie's Father* – this may take the form of a 'romance' between a parent and a child.

It is striking just how many of the films we'll be looking at include as part of their subject matter precisely those issues to which a study of the melodramatic, the comedic and the romantic leads, exploring, in particular, the shifts and ambiguities amongst them (as in the theatrical troupe's debates, in *To Be or Not to Be*, over whether to go for realism or comedy in their productions, or as in *The Palm Beach Story*'s questioning of whether couples *do* live happily ever after, once they are married). This is further exemplified by the two quotations which preface this chapter, from *The Miracle of Morgan's Creek* and *Once upon a Honeymoon*, with their respective meditations on how a small town can be either oppressive or sheltering and how it's not always easy to predict which it will be, and how, even in a comedy, there may be no safe place for at least some of its marginal characters. *To Catch a Thief*, as well, has demonstrated an interest in the processes by which narrative and social conventions may combine to suppress the desires of some of its characters (for example, middle-aged mothers); the resultant disturbance to the film's resolution in this case is humorously encapsulated in Francie's final throwaway remark – 'Oh, mother will love it up here!' – when she's snared Robie for herself.

In identifying some of these issues, and in discovering the abundance and complexity of meaning in the films I have selected, it is useful to consider what George M. Wilson calls 'rhetorical figures of narrational instruction' (in *Narration in Light: Studies in Cinematic Point of View*, The Johns Hopkins University Press, 1986, p.49) which are 'found so commonly in complex, interesting films. Some paradigm is needed to ostend those objects, properties, and relations, out of all that appear on screen, that are to have a weighted explanatory function in the film' (p.50). Examples of such rhetorical strategies, which will be examined more closely later, range from the melodramatic – as in the sight of Louise Avery (Barbara Rush), in *Bigger than Life*, hesitating in a frozen pose on the threshold of a darkened room as her husband, Ed, collapses offscreen, to the comedic – like the moment in *Monkey Business* (Howard Hawks, 1952) when the space of the narrative world itself seems to open up to accommodate the safe passage of Barnaby Fulton (Cary Grant) in his wildly careening car, and on to the romantic – when stars shine in the eyes of Geraldine Jeffers, in *The Palm Beach Story*, as she thinks of her husband Tom, or when his hands on her hips provide a steadying counter-influence to her impetuosity as she once more throws in her lot with his. One might also call to mind the final moments of *Brigadoon* when the romantic couple is reunited in the middle of Brigadoon's hundred-year-long night, and Fiona (Cyd Charisse) appears at the open door of her cottage silhouetted by the light in the doorway behind her. Here the cinematic nature of Tommy's romantic fulfilment is displayed and held for an instant in a sort of magical suspension just before Fiona steps tentatively out towards Tommy, her figure seemingly projected into the darkness on a beam of light.

American movies are rich in such instructional moments, their images and ways of imagining intimately linked. As we've just seen, these moments may indicate a film's repressiveness and the struggles for power within its narrative world or, alternatively, its tolerant generosity and expansiveness. Through the imagery of such rhetorical figures, a clash between these two fundamental ways of being a film may be played out as opposing configurations in space, their resolution mirrored in a kind of spatial balance or symmetry, as in the final moments of *The Courtship of Eddie's Father*, when Eddie orchestrates his father's reconciliation with Elizabeth as he stands in the hallway between their two apartments and watches them talk on the telephone. Sometimes, all we may get is the merest hint of a better world, captured for an instant in a glance or a smile, as in the momentary laughter of John Robie and Jessie Stevens, shared across a gaming table in the south of France, or in the saturated yellow of the robe worn by Feodor Sverdlov (Omar Sharif) as he introduces himself to Judith Farrow (Julie Andrews) in *The Tamarind Seed* (Blake Edwards, 1974), with its promise of sexual intensity and warmth.

It should be clear by now that my concern is not to define or analyse any of the standard genres anew, nor to try to determine how specific melodramatic and comic genres have been or might be designated. If there is any originality in my account, it lies at another level. I began, simply, with a very broad sense of difference between the melodramatic and the comedic, in terms of something like Christine Gledhill's assumption of a melodramatic 'way of viewing the world' or Gerald Mast's assumption of a 'comic climate'. Along with many other writers and viewers, I share a sense of the repressiveness of the melodramatic and the playful disruption of the comedic, which directly affects our own bodily states as spectators anticipating such films. For example, preparing to watch a film whose narrative world is as repressive as that of *Schindler's List* requires a very different state of readiness from the physical and mental relaxation which accompanies the anticipation of a comedic film: this is by no means a judgment as to the value of the film, of course, but an assumption about the nature of the experience we will be invited to undergo in our viewing. However, such expectations may well be mistaken, particularly if based on generic signals alone. Where our assumptions are reinforced by a consistent and powerful rhetoric in the publicity for a film and in accounts of its reception, we may be so blinkered to other possibilities that, even after seeing the film, our awareness of conflicting effects is suppressed. A good example of this, as we'll see in the concluding section of Chapter Four, is *The Sound of Music* (Robert Wise, 1965), a film whose melodramatic repressiveness is often overlooked by those who return to it as a straightforward source of romantic and comedic pleasures.

To the extent that I had an initial hypothesis, it was this: where the repressiveness of the melodramatic seems to be partly a result of its reproduction of the hierarchies of power and status which structure our own world outside the films, the playfulness of the comedic seems to flourish to the extent that this world can be imaginatively transformed. Although the domain of American films can be mapped at many levels and in terms of many categorical schemes, my contention is that the opposition between the melodramatic and the comedic, and the ways in which romance is inflected by each, are fundamental and illuminating.

CHAPTER TWO

MELODRAMATIC MASCULINITIES

INCREDIBLE SHRINKING MEN

> *'Lonesome' Rhodes (Andy Griffith):* See what I mean? The bigger I get, the smaller you make me feel . . .
>> Rhodes to Marcia Jeffries (Patricia Neal) in *A Face in the Crowd* (Elia Kazan, 1957)

> *Bridget (Linda Fiorentino):* What's so special about me?
> *Mike (Peter Berg):* You've been out there. You came here and you chose me.
> *Bridget:* So?
> *Mike:* So I was right, I'm bigger than this town.
> *Bridget:* So what's wrong?
> *Mike:* You can't stop reminding me that you're bigger than me.
>> *The Last Seduction* (John Dahl, 1993)

I want now to take a closer look at a number of specific films which, although from a variety of genres (science fiction, domestic melodrama, the war film), are all broadly melodramatic in structure and mood. In particular, I wish to explore their treatment of the theme of 'becoming a man' which draws both on male-centred fantasies of augmentation and diminishment within the domestic space and on a flight into violence elsewhere. In many ways, of course, fantasies of augmentation and diminishment are two sides of the same coin, for the fear of being little is the nightmare fantasy which fuels its opposite, the dream of being big. So a film like *The Incredible Shrinking Man* – or, indeed, *Attack of the 50 Foot Woman* (Nathan Hertz [Juran], 1958), with the identical image of a mismatched married couple in which the wife towers over the husband – is part of the same thematic as *Bigger than Life*, though the latter seems a more clear-cut case, at first glance, of a fantasy of augmentation, as its title indicates. Before moving on to the two films which form the central focus of this chapter, a brief discussion of *The Incredible Shrinking Man* may help to set the scene.

This film is both less coherent and more baldly schematic than either *Bigger than Life* or *Schindler's List*, but it nonetheless provides a useful introduction to some of the same concerns. Its thematic links with *Bigger than Life* are especially clear. One of the difficulties in working out the film's position, however, is that the narrative is centred to such an extent upon the views and consciousness of the central male character, Scott Carey (Grant Williams), through his voice-over narration and the fact that once he has escaped from his pet cat into the basement he spends the greater part of the film away from other people. The film does little to distance us from his analysis

The Incredible Shrinking Man. Lou (Randy Stuart) towers over Scott (Grant Williams).

of his predicament or his remarkable face-saving narration which allows him to see his diminishment as augmentation ('So close, the infinitesimal and the infinite. But suddenly I knew they were really the two ends of the same concept. The unbelievably small and the unbelievably vast eventually meet like the closing of a gigantic circle').

Scott's problems begin while he is on holiday with his wife Lou (Randy Stuart), who, incidentally, has the same name as the wife in *Bigger than Life*. Both husband and wife are lounging in the sun on the deck of a boat provided by his evidently more successful brother Charlie (Paul Langton). A playful argument develops when he insists she get him a cold beer and she refuses, until he promises to get dinner that evening in return. While she's below deck, a strange radioactive mist envelops Scott and seals his fate, though his shrinking is not apparent until six months later. More than one possible reading of his 'disease' seems to be offered by the film: the doctor initially blames overwork and worry, and suggests he's not eating well, yet the fact that Scott has been contaminated while on holiday belies this, unless we allow him an unconscious desire to prolong his absence from work indefinitely by refusing such responsibilities altogether (his diminishment, in this sense, a literal shrinking from

The Incredible Shrinking Man. The cat gets in; Scott falls to the basement.

responsibility). Indeed, Scott himself has a moment of apparent insight when he later readies himself for a struggle to the death with the spider in the basement: 'A strange calm possessed me. I thought more clearly than I had ever thought before, as if my mind were bathed in a brilliant light. I recognised that part of my illness was rooted in hunger.' Understood metaphorically, this implies Scott's emotional neediness as much as his physical hunger, and it is suggestively linked to Lou's refusal to get him a beer – and his agreement to get dinner himself – in the opening scene. The film, however, gives us little help in deciding whether the illness represents Lou's revenge on Scott for expecting her to serve and obey him (allowing us the possibility of a feminist appropriation of the film from Lou's perspective) or whether Scott is being punished by the film for not being manly enough in insisting on his 'rights', or, indeed, as already suggested, whether Scott's illness is a rather drastic escape from domestic responsibilities altogether. In each of these cases, however, it seems evident that Lou is unprepared to meet his needs and that his resultant 'hunger' and 'undernourishment' diminish him in both a metaphoric and a literal sense. So marital conflict appears to generate Scott's predicament, which can be seen as providing either a punishment or an escape or both.

A crucial turn for the worse in Scott's situation – and a critical turning point in the film – is when his fall to the basement of his home forces him to withdraw completely from human contact. By this stage, he is so small that he is living in a doll's house in the living room and, as Lou sets out for the corner store, he reminds her to 'be sure the doors are locked'. However, when she briefly returns to the house to collect something she's left behind, she leaves the door ajar, and this lapse (which can easily be read as a Freudian parapraxis, especially given the blatant way it follows, and disregards, Scott's anxious warning) allows the cat to get in and threaten Scott's life. As Lou is going out, and before he realises that he is in danger, Scott muses on his worsening behaviour to Lou: 'Every day it was worse. Every day a little smaller. And every day I became more tyrannical, more monstrous in my domination of Louise.' On Lou's return, despite the evidence of the open cellar door, she is quick to believe him dead, and the scene shifts, for most of the remainder of the film, to Scott's tribulations in the basement, a world he resolves to dominate.

His main opponent is a black spider and – given the way it displaces Lou as his rival for food and nourishment and as the intended object of his domination, as well as the unseemly haste with which Lou has accepted that Scott is dead (her later doubts easily silenced by Charlie's persuasiveness) – the film's logic appears to require us to take it as a 'black widow'. It is thus Lou's representative, at least in Scott's fantasies, in the basement underworld he now inhabits, a world he first entered in an unconscious state when he was knocked down the stairs by the cellar door blowing open as Lou came in through the front door of the house on her return from the store. Thus, Scott's description of his relationship with the spider – 'In my hunt for food, I had become the hunted. This time I survived, but I was no longer alone in my universe. I had an enemy, the most terrifying ever beheld by human eyes' – is followed by a dissolve to his brother and Lou upstairs as she prepares to leave, abandoning him to his fate. When the spider returns, Scott continues to reflect along similar lines: 'My enemy seemed immortal. More than a spider it was every unknown terror in the world, every fear fused into one hideous night-black horror', his words making even more clear the spider's function as the place of projection of his wider fears. 'Still,' he adds, 'whatever else had happened, my brain was a man's brain, my intelligence still a man's intelligence,' and this insistence confirms our suspicions that gender conflict is at the heart of his problems, and his 'manhood' the matter at issue.

Nonetheless, the film does little with these central thematic concerns except to permit Scott a Pyrrhic victory over the spider, which he stabs to death before he dwindles into nothingness. This is an extraordinary ending in a science fiction movie of the 'fifties: our expectations – that Lou will discover Scott in the basement, that medical science will triumph, however provisionally, and that Scott will survive, or at least die with a semblance of resistance to his fate – are all confounded by the film's unmitigated downward spiral of defeat. Scott's quasi-religious eagerness to accept and rationalise his destiny ('To God there is no zero. I still exist') suggests the extent to which other ways out are blocked. By moving Scott into so threadbare a symbolic battlefield away from the complexities of human contact and the social domain, where much of interest could have been said about masculinity in 'fifties America, the film has painted itself into a corner.

The issues which *Bigger than Life* takes on with such a sharp and unflinching eye seem pushed to the sidelines here, though the fact that they are present is still of interest. For example, like Ed Avery in *Bigger than Life*, Scott is presented not just as hungry, but as a child. When he first begins to lose weight, Lou's response makes this clear: 'Ah, well, that does it, my boy, you're going to start taking vitamins. I'll get you so fat on ice-cream and cake you'll think you're living in a child's paradise'; and his description of himself as he continues to shrink, 'The child that looks like a man' (rather than the more accurate 'man who looks like a child'), also implies that he is really a child, with only the appearance of adult masculinity, rather than its substance. There is also at least a hint that his diminishment threatens to feminise him as well. Thus, when he walks past the sideshow and hears the barker's description of Tiny Tina, a midget, he covers his ears as though the description applies to *him*: 'Thirty-six and a half inches of feminine pulchritude . . .' Later, in the basement after it has been flooded by the burst water-heater and blocked drain, when Scott tries to get the attention of Lou and Charlie, his voice goes unheard. But, despite all these references to a gendered and hierarchical social domain, and Scott's increasing power-lessness within it, the film – with Scott – beats a hasty retreat to the basement and resolves its conflicts in abstract and religiously mystified symbolism which is un-anchored in any perspective larger than the facile and self-serving perspective of Scott himself, leaving us to take this at face value.

As melodrama has usually been construed as being centred upon female characters and experiences, and I have concentrated on male melodramatic fantasies, my example may be attacked as unrepresentative. My response to this is two-fold. Firstly, although melodrama in its traditional generic sense has been seen as centred around female characters, the melodramatic as a category which cuts across genres includes at least as many films centred on men and male experience: *film noir*, the Western, the war film, horror and science fiction provide many of the best examples of the melodramatic in its broadest sense. Secondly, however, I would argue that even so-called female-centred melodramas are much more determined by male fantasies and anxieties than has generally been acknowledged. In *The Incredible Shrinking Man*,

Scott's most spectacular dramas take place in a space apart (the basement), while his wife Lou gets on with her life upstairs. A shift in point of view from Scott to Lou – which would transform the film into an example of a female-centred domestic melodrama – would push Scott 'offstage' and construct him merely as an absence, for the viewer as well as for Lou. Indeed, numerous female-centred domestic melodramas do just this by concentrating on a woman whose husband is dead or elsewhere: for example, *Since You Went Away* (John Cromwell, 1944), *The Reckless Moment* (Max Ophuls, 1949), *All That Heaven Allows* (Douglas Sirk, 1956), *Imitation of Life* (Douglas Sirk, 1959) and many more. Such films, while female-centred, are nonetheless part of a larger context in which female fantasies of independence and strength (and the corresponding anxieties about powerlessness which give them their force) mesh with the same male fears of diminishment at the hands of women (and their corresponding fantasies of revenge) that underpin *The Incredible Shrinking Man*. Absence and death, after all, are the ultimate diminishments, as Scott Carey finds out. That such absence is ambiguous, I have already pointed out: it may be seen as a punishment of the male character at the hands of a woman or at the hands of the film itself or it may be self-willed. Thus, in films like *Shock Corridor* (Samuel Fuller, 1963) and *Torn Curtain* (Alfred Hitchcock, 1966), the male protagonist's flight into a mental hospital (and his subsequent madness) in the former case, and behind the Iron Curtain in the latter, can both be seen as flights from strong and demanding women. Hitchcock's title – *Torn Curtain* – is suggestive not only of the central male character's penetration of the Communist world, but of an attempted escape from the domestic world in the process.

Female-centred films which diminish men or push them offscreen and male-centred films of escape from the domestic where men fear such diminishment are emphasising different halves of the same thematic whole, as are films which concentrate on female fears of powerlessness and those centred on male fantasies of augmentation: that is, the difficulties of sustaining positive heterosexual relationships in a social context where there is an unequal distribution of power between the sexes. As I have indicated above, female-centred films and their fantasies of power are likely to involve anxieties about powerlessness; similarly, male-centred fantasies of augmentation are shadowed by fears of diminishment. Whether such films are seen to focus on male or female fantasies and anxieties depends on a range of issues linked closely to structures of identification and point of view, but male and female fantasies about heterosexual relationships are clearly complementary and, even where one of them appears to be absent or is underplayed, it is often at least implicitly there. *Bigger than Life* is an excellent example of a film which – though centred on Ed – gives considerable force and presence to his wife's anxieties and fantasies of revenge, which interlock with his. In contrast, *The Incredible Shrinking Man* suppresses Lou's perspective at an early stage, reducing her to little more than a fantasy figure for Scott, symbolically embodied in the spider he destroys.

Even when concerns about becoming or failing to become a man in traditional terms are thematically central, films vary both in their sympathies and in the specific locations which are given prominence on screen, whether these are domestic settings or alternative spaces elsewhere. There are examples of comparable female figures who are ejected by men from the domestic space, by being killed (as with Rebecca – though it's not strictly murder – in Alfred Hitchcock's 1940 film of that name) or sequestered (as with Jessica/Christine Gordon in Jacques Tourneur's 1943 film, *I Walked with a Zombie*) or, much more occasionally, by willingly fleeing, but these women tend to strive to return, whereas their male counterparts tend to strive to stay away. Because of this, we are less likely to follow such women out of the domestic space than we are to accompany their male counterparts in their flights away. In addition, such films often replace the absent woman in the domestic setting with another woman who becomes the central female figure of identification for women viewers. The so-called madwoman in the attic is involuntarily absent from the film's centre stage, whereas the madman in the basement (as it were) is usually voluntarily absent or on the run. *Psycho* is an interesting conflation of both scenarios, as Mrs Bates/Norman (Anthony Perkins) is ambiguously female *and* male and, though usually kept upstairs in the Gothic mansion on the hill, is, when required, also hidden away in its fruit cellar.

I have argued that, in general, the melodramatic 'elsewhere' is a male fantasy space which functions as a refuge from the threat of diminishment within the domestic space of the normal social world (as embodied in marriage, home, the small town, 'civilisation', and so forth). Since sexual desire is the lure which fixes men within the domestic domain, the melodramatic flight away is also a flight from the entanglements of desire itself when this is perceived as entailing settlement and domestication. Thus, the city of *film noir* may entice its protagonists away from small-town domesticity through the promise of a freer sexuality with no strings attached. However, the consequences of such relationships may prove to be just as dangerous as 'settling down', the *femme fatale* often threatening the male protagonist with a distorted and magnified version of the disempowerment feared in small-town marriage. In the case of the *femme fatale*, however, her blatant infidelities and betrayals license the male protagonist to turn his violence or vengeful fantasies on her, providing a narrative release which would not be sanctioned in a small-town romance. Pushing this somewhat further, the source of the attraction of the *femme fatale* may well be inherently sadistic, given the freedom her bad behaviour seems to provide to her would-be lover to act out such violent fantasies against her, converting desire for the 'good' woman back home (and the resultant disguised aggression towards her) into more direct and permissible punishment of her transgressive stand-in. Where the so-called 'bad' woman turns out to be 'good', her lover's sadism is all the more blatantly exposed (Alfred Hitchcock's *Notorious*, 1946, provides a particularly clear example).

The wide open spaces of the Western and the battlegrounds of the war film provide landscapes which are generally much more free of sexual complications than the sullied cityscapes of *film noir*, but they may equally be seen as providing possiblities for escape from both women and home. However, the targets of male aggression here – the Western's Indians and the war film's enemies – are not sadistically eroticised in the same way as the *femme fatale* (in any case, not as overtly). My analysis of *Bigger than Life* is followed by a close look at *Schindler's List* (not quite a war film, with its battlefield transformed to the forced-labour camp of Plaszów), to explore whether and in what ways the underlying concerns of both films are related, despite obvious differences of genre and intention. In the course of this investigation, I will return to the questions sketched out earlier: what is the nature of the melodramatic, and how much variation can it accommodate without loss of coherence?

Bigger than Life

Nicholas Ray's film charts the illness of a struggling schoolteacher, Ed Avery (James Mason), and his psychotic behaviour provoked by unregulated use of the drug cortisone which carries him to the brink of killing his son Richie (Christopher Olsen), his wife Lou (Barbara Rush) and himself. The film's title, *Bigger than Life*, is charged with meaning. In common with a raft of other 'fifties films, with their widescreen format and vivid colour, the movie promises – in this case, through its title – an experience for its viewers which is truly bigger than life, or, at any rate, bigger than television and the domestic routines within which the experience of television is embedded. Indeed, television functions within the film both to emphasise the drudgery of the ordinary ('Doesn't this stuff bore you?' Ed asks Richie; 'It's always the same story') and as an accompaniment to Ed's attempted murder of his son. Ed switches on the television before going upstairs, as though its images of a fairground ride going round in endless circles – an increasingly frenzied repetition – are a necessary final spur to his intended actions. The film itself, like the altered states of its central character, takes us out of what he disparagingly refers to as 'petty domesticity' and encourages us to share Ed's desire for something more grandiose and less constrained. Even the *mise en scène*, with its frequent splashes of orange and red, reflects the arterial inflammation of Ed's disease, the external and internal aspects of this feverish intensity conjoined at the moment when the film represents Ed's pained consciousness, as he's about to kill his son, by a red suffusion of the screen. If television is complicit in Ed's attempted murder of his son – being at the very least exemplary of the repetitive and colourless world he is reacting against and which spurs him to action, then colour may be said to come to the rescue, as Richie dashes past the stricken Ed to safety. Ed's momentary paralysis, at this point, is precipitated by Richie's holding out to his father the football representing Ed's small-scale high-school heroics, which may imply that Richie's refusal to be a willing heir to such masculine mettle – his insistence on being a child – has the power to stop his father in his tracks. Alternatively, it may represent Richie's attempt at propitiation, as Victor Perkins has suggested to me, with Richie implicitly agreeing to play football as the price of survival. However, on either reading, what's clear is that Richie has no desire to play football, and that 'being a man' in these terms gives him no joy.

I have argued that *Bigger than Life* invites us to enjoy the excesses of a widescreen colour melodrama, but its title also – and more obviously – points us in the direction of Ed's exaggerated masculine hubris while under the influence of cortisone, then a largely experimental drug whose side-effects were not fully understood. Thus, Ed tells Lou that he felt 'ten feet tall' when he saw her and Richie waiting for him on his release from hospital – an ambiguous reaction, given his later claim to have outgrown his wife, a process clearly already at work. His colleague, Wally (Walter Matthau), later complains to Lou that Ed has changed: 'You know – big shot – he even *looks* bigger.' But, of course, Ed is not ten feet tall, and the use of such metaphors suggests the illusory nature of his perceived augmentation. If 'life' is what is real, then a man who is 'bigger' than life is clearly not to be trusted, a false god waiting to be toppled. Ed's high-school football provides an evocative parallel: a reminder of his sudden and altogether arbitrary elevation to glory ('Third-string sub to hero in twenty seconds'), it is shown in an early scene limp, deflated and in need of pumping up. Heroic masculinity, whether it arrives through the 'miracle' of a moment of fame arbitrarily given to a third-rate footballer or is effected by a 'miracle' drug gone wrong, is an illusion, and its bestowal, as with all miracles, is in the gift of the gods (or, in the case of the drug, of doctors – the film's secular gods).

So a third way of interpreting the film's title is as a reference to patriarchy itself, by which I understand a form of social regulation whose structures and institutions privilege men over women, even if individual men don't always feel its benefits, as in Ed Avery's case where patriarchy's representatives and requirements seem to control his life from all quarters. This is what Ed challenges, under the influence of the drug, trying to usurp the places and status of a range of controlling males. Thus, after Ed's arrogant speech at the PTA meeting, when an approving parent tells the school Principal – Ed's boss, La Porte (Rusty Lane) – that Ed should be Principal, there is a close-up of Ed reacting with smug satisfaction. Similarly, he appropriates his doctors' role by impersonating a doctor in order to get extra supplies of the drug, and later denounces the minister's sermon, taking on his role as well, leading to his stunning declaration (when Lou challenges his interpretation of the story of Abraham and Isaac) that 'God was wrong'. However, while Ed seeks to become more patriarchal than God himself, Richie seeks, as we've seen, to hold on to his childhood by resisting as far as he can his father's wish that he excel at football ('You want to be a man, don't you?' Ed had asked when Richie flagged during their football practice together). Richie is thus accepting his powerlessness, as well as refusing illusory power – an accommodation with patriarchy. Similarly, a fundamental aspect of Ed's dilemma is his own inability to extricate himself from such hierarchies of power.

Ed occupies three conflicting positions: his normal state before illness strikes; the illness into which he rapidly falls; and the cortisone-induced psychosis which follows. The film barely shows him in the first of these conditions, merely hinting at it in the shot of his desk at school, with watch and keys proclaiming him a prisoner of time and domestic responsibilities, before his hand stiffens in pain as the first attack takes place. Thus, he is a man already ill, the early attacks seemingly triggered by his responsibilities at work (both at school and at the taxi company where he moonlights) and at home (during and after the bridge evening organised by his wife). The first attack is preceded by the opening shots of the film as, to an initially ominous musical accompaniment which then lightens up, we approach the school, and a stream of pupils rush out for the start of the Easter vacation, a number of them dressed partly, and strikingly, in red. Several ideas are condensed here: the sense of release as the children escape, in contrast to Ed and the boy he's detained inside, and the links (via the accents of red in the children's clothing, which anticipate Ed's inflammation of the arteries, itself an expression of his more general pain) between the children and Ed, suggesting the mismatch between their desires and the fate which awaits them as adults, but also suggesting the child within Ed. This symbolism will soon be concentrated more specifically on Richie, through his red jacket, but at this point Ed is both on the side of the children generally and childlike himself. This is clear in his treatment of Joe, the boy in detention.

After his pain attack in the classroom has subsided, Ed asks Joe to name the Great Lakes but, when it's clear that the child is at a loss, he settles for just one, smiling with genuine pleasure when Joe manages to come up with Lake Huron, and advising him that he can catch up with the other children outside if he runs. Again, this episode is tightly packed in its significance. The reference to the Great Lakes reinforces the film title's concern with size. It is worth noting here that, in a later classroom scene after his release from the hospital, Ed asks the same child, 'In your own words, why did Cassius refer to Julius Caesar as a colossus?' which reiterates this pre-occupation, but also affiliates Caesar's epilepsy – his falling sickness – with the attack Ed has after the bridge party when he falls down unconscious. These references to size and grandeur are reflected in the images that decorate Ed's home – specifically the posters of the Grand Canyon and Rome – but they also set up an opposition between natural and cultural magnitude and power (the Great Lakes and the Grand Canyon versus Caesar and Rome). That battle lines must be drawn between them is most forcefully argued in Ed's speech to the parents at the PTA meeting, when – under the growing influence of cortisone – he contrasts what are assumed to be 'the unspoiled instincts of childhood' with 'hard work, and self-discipline and a sense of duty' which he sees as necessary to contain these instincts, emphasising the cultural littleness of children ('we're breeding a race of moral midgets'). By this point, Ed considers that 'childhood is a congenital disease' and that a repressive and controlling patriarchal culture and his alignment with such values and controlling figures will provide the cure. But, in the opening scene, he is still on the side of childhood, identifying with its vulnerability as well as its less acculturated state. It is worth noting that, when Ed has to leave the classroom, after asking Joe the question about Julius Caesar, and he puts the boy in charge of the class, Joe takes great satisfaction in posing the same question to another child, thus saving face at his own lack of success by taking on, with considerable relish, the teacher's role, as Ed will take on the roles of his oppressors later on.

Joe's forgetting of the names of the Great Lakes is an indication of the even greater extent to which internalised 'nature' (that is, desires, anger and so on) is repressed in normal adults: like the Great Lakes, it can hardly be named. And yet the naming of Lake Huron is no more than an instance of rote memory, a naming of something perceived by Joe as extraneous and irrelevant to his own concerns, reducing him to a dutiful, if somewhat embarrassed, automaton, who lacks sufficient insight to enable him to appropriate the realm of nature – at least in the form of his anger or resentment – as his own. Similarly, when Ed's condition is diagnosed using medical Latin (perhaps the nearest he will get to Caesar or to Rome), all control is wrested from him; his disease is no longer his – that is to say, it is no longer an expression of a pain which belongs to him and reflects his material condition within society and the home, but, rather, something extraneous which must be eliminated (or repressed) so that he will return to the dutiful absent-mindedness which characterises him in the film's early scenes. This sense Ed gives of being elsewhere – of not paying due attention to the everyday world and tasks which surround him – can be seen in his own forgetfulness; he can't, for example, remember what he'd promised Lou he'd bring home for the party (olives, as it turns out). But also, more interestingly, it can be seen in another trait which links Ed to childhood in the opening scenes: his obliviousness to sexual innuendo. Thus, the obvious interest taken in him by a fellow teacher, Pat (Kipp Hamilton), is completely lost on him – at least on a conscious level – as are

Lou's sarcastic comment when he tells her that Wally is considering bringing Pat with him to the bridge party ('I thought she only played hearts') and the atmosphere of sexual jealousy which permeates Lou's brief meeting with Pat in the kitchen.

Ed's comment, later in the film, when he and Lou embrace after an argument – 'We've been away from each other too long' – reveals the sexlessness of their marriage. Reading this back into the film's early scenes, the reasons behind Lou's ready resentments and suspicions become much more complex. The habitual form that her resentment takes, however, is frustration at the couple's economically straitened circumstances, which only adds to the pressure on Ed to continue to supplement their income with his job at the taxi firm, whose 'unworthiness' in Lou's eyes is the cause of Ed's secrecy in the early part of the film. This, in turn, provokes Lou's suspicions of sexual infidelity on Ed's part, thus further estranging them while her resentment grows. Ed seems scarcely aware of this vicious circle, yet it rules Lou's world. One has only to compare Ed's complete lack of embarrassment when he has to borrow his bus fare from his boss, with Lou's mortification – however she tries to disguise it – when a salesman calls at the house on behalf of the dress shop to sort out the bad cheque Ed had signed. Even at the climax of the film, when Lou tries to forestall Ed's attempt to murder Richie by showing him their son's baby photographs, she seems unable to resist a throwaway reference to his inability to provide for them: 'You're pushing him in that awful second-hand baby carriage.' Here Ed averts his eyes. 'Now look, Ed.'

Lou resents both her absolute economic dependence upon her husband and his inability to support her adequately, even where fairly basic middle-class comforts are concerned (he cannot protect her from anxiety over a broken water-heater, say), but 1950s America offers her no way out. Thus, when Wally suggests that Lou might 'carry the ball' for a while – an interesting metaphor in view of the significance given to Ed's football as a sign of his manliness – she is suitably dismissive ('Do you think Ed would let me go out and earn a living while he's in the hospital?'), and her lack of independent economic status makes her extremely sensitive to perceived slights regarding her capabilities. Thus, when one of the taxi drivers who works with Ed visits him in hospital, and Ed responds to Lou's puzzlement by stating the obvious, 'He's a cab-driver', her reply, while jokey, is barely able to conceal a reprimand of Ed for his implied belittlement of her intelligence: 'Oh, I'd never have known'. This defensiveness emerges more aggressively when she challenges Dr Norton (Robert Simon) near the end of the film: 'I am not precisely an idiot. What are you hiding?' Her remark gains further emphasis insofar as it follows on from Lou's attempt to get the attention of a nurse who proceeds to ignore her, a moment clearly reminiscent of the scene in the expensive dress shop when a saleswoman had snubbed Ed in his attempt to buy Lou a dress and he had threatened to make an issue of it. So if Ed's conscious resentment at his belittlement is less developed than Lou's at the start of the film, he becomes increasingly inflamed – both physically and emotionally – as his disease takes hold. The disease gives him an opportunity to express his pain and anger, but not to cure them. And, rather than uniting Ed and Lou in a shared awareness of the extent to which external circumstances oppress them both, it serves only to drive them further apart as each increasingly sees the other as principal oppressor.

A recurring motif which underlines their growing mutual alienation is the closing of doors, which compartmentalises them in separate spaces and, in some

Bigger than Life.
'Bring me anything?'
Ed (James Mason)
and Richie
(Christopher Olsen).

instances, suggests the strengthening alliance of Lou and Richie against Ed (Richie's first words to his father in the film – 'Bring me anything?' – imply that he too, like his mother, is a constant reminder to Ed of his limitations as provider). Even at the bridge party early on, we discover Lou and Ed in separate rooms. When Lou goes to the kitchen, it is less to be with Ed than to dislodge Pat, and she closes the kitchen door on Ed as she returns to her guests shortly afterwards. When Wally takes Ed to hospital, Richie closes the front door on himself and his mother as his father is driven off. Examples proliferate in the later stages of the film: Ed closing the bedroom door on Lou before going to phone Dr Norton (though he hangs up when he sees the outstanding bills by the telephone), Richie locking himself in the bathroom, away from his father, Ed shutting Richie in his bedroom and locking Lou in a closet, and so on. Given the fact that, by then, they seem barely able to endure being in the same room with each other, the final scene – Richie, Lou and Ed together in the hospital room, the door closed on the rest of the world outside – is claustrophobic, to say the least.

This may be a useful place to recapitulate the argument so far. I have suggested that Ed, like the 'poor bewildered kids' he describes at the PTA meeting, begins as an absent-minded, but dutiful, husband whose rebellious desire for something bigger and better than just making do slips out only symptomatically: in his forgetting the olives for Lou, in the travel posters at his home, in occasional good-natured comments about the repetitiveness of television, the dullness of his life, the fact that his job at the taxi company 'pays the bills', and so forth. But ultimately his resentment surfaces with greatest force in his attacks of pain. Lou's resentment is more conscious and overt,

Bigger than Life. Lou (Barbara Rush): 'I'm supposed to be dull, remember?' She pauses on the threshold of the bedroom after the thud of Ed falling. Ed lying on the floor.

perhaps because her position is even less tenable than Ed's. This resentment becomes more aggressive, not less, in response to Ed's illness and her growing panic – not just at the shabbiness and shame of being the wife of a poor provider, but at the prospect of total economic abandonment if he becomes permanently unable to work. His forgetting to bring her the olives is arguably 'answered', as he sets off for the hospital, by her forgetting to give him his slippers (an apt symbol of the domestic comfort she unconsciously withholds), but his limitations as breadwinner when they are unable to afford a new water-heater and she must repeatedly boil the kettle to fill his bath, are dealt with much more consciously and with greater violence when she slams shut the bathroom cabinet, shattering the mirror and his reflection within it.

Indeed, Ed's devastating attack of pain after the bridge party – which leads to his hospitalisation – can be understood not just as the final surfacing of Ed's previously repressed resentment, but as a punishment directed towards him from outside, that is, from Lou. At this point her panic about being economically abandoned is at its peak, as she is convinced he's romantically involved with someone else.

> *Ed:* Let's face it, we're dull.
> *Lou:* Have you found somebody who isn't?
> *Ed:* What do you mean by that?
> *Lou:* There was no Board meeting. Where were you?
> *Ed:* I told you. What did you think I was doing?
> *Lou:* Well, you can't expect me to figure that out. I'm supposed to be dull, remember?
> *Ed:* I said we *all* are. [*He turns away, but continues speaking as she then turns away in the opposite direction.*] Can you tell me one thing that was said or done by anyone here tonight that was funny, startling, imaginative?'

As Lou opens the door to Richie's bedroom and is about to go through it into the darkened room, her back to the camera, the thud of Ed falling is heard. Her averted posture at the moment of Ed's offscreen fall is one of several instances of 'looking away' in the film, often associated with Lou guiltily acting out her own interests at Ed's expense. For example, when, in view of Ed's increasingly erratic behaviour, Wally wants Lou to get help for him, she turns her back on Wally in the course of replying: 'Wally, Wally, mind your own business. No matter how close we are to the La Portes socially, Bob is still his boss. And we mustn't let him think that Ed's still sick. He may force Ed to take a vacation. Do you have any idea what that would mean? Just the cortisone Ed

has to take costs $2 a day.' However, as already mentioned, Ed, too, averts his eyes from the photograph of Richie in his baby carriage, and Richie himself averts his body and, initially, his face too, when he holds out the football to his father near the end of the film, thereby provoking Ed's paralysing attack, as Lou appears to have done when she turns to go into Richie's bedroom. Ironically, Ed's claim earlier in the evening that no one has done anything 'startling' or 'imaginative' is no longer the case.

The idea that Lou wills Ed to fall gains further support by the throaty sensuality of her initial response – 'Ed?' – as she turns around after he has fallen, and the way she seems to savour the moment as she stands in the doorway for an instant, framed by the bedroom's darkness behind her, before remembering herself and rushing to his side, repeating his name in a more appropriately worried tone of voice. For, whatever her resentment, her dilemma remains: the desire to destroy Ed for his anticipated abandonment of her would clearly defeat its purpose, producing a far more thoroughgoing abandonment if he dies. After Lou tells Richie to telephone the doctor, her afterthought as she kneels beside Ed – 'And call Uncle Wally, too' – is more than a little chilling in its suggestion that she may be hedging her bets by lining up an alternative future breadwinner. That Lou is dressed in black – inappropriate both for the season and the occasion (to judge by the clothes of everyone else at the bridge party) – indicates to us that, even if she is not yet a widow, she is already dressing the part.

The mutually reinforcing connotations of absent-mindedness, forgetting and averting one's gaze which characterise Ed and his family feed into our reading of these events. Though the examples of forgetting already mentioned are relatively trivial (the olives, the slippers, the names of the Great Lakes), three further examples of lapses in memory or understanding are much more heavily marked by the film and, taken in conjunction, suggest a wish on the part of all three – not only Lou and Richie, but Ed himself – to see him dead. The film's first instance of this is when Ed, having commented to his doctors that he can't afford any more symptoms, prepares to leave hospital to go home, only to be recalled at the door by Dr Norton: 'Ed, you forgot your pills.' Similarly, after Ed has begun to bully Richie, and Wally has told Lou of the dangerous side-effects of cortisone, Lou tells Ed he must not take the drug any more, suddenly stopping as she realises that this would mean his death.

> *Ed:* Yes? Did you forget what you were going to say?
> *Lou:* I forgot.

When Richie tells Lou that he hates his father, she explains that the pills are to blame but that Ed can't stop taking them or his terrible pain will return ('Now we wouldn't want that to happen, would we?'), and Richie replies that 'I just didn't get it.' But when his father's dictatorial behaviour continues, Richie tries to find and destroy the cortisone the next day after church, telling his father that 'I'd rather you were dead than the way you are now'. It is in reaction to Richie's 'theft' of the pills that Ed settles on the murder of his son, and the joint suicide of Lou and himself in its wake ('There's nothing left for us to live for now'). It is precisely because Ed's options are so limited that his death begins to appear to all of them as the only way out.

The web of murderous desires which pervades the Avery household – despite the efforts of its members to deny them through claims of forgetfulness and inattention

– is reflected metaphorically in the shadows that they trail behind them as they watch each other in an atmosphere of increasing distrust which, in most instances, is fully justified. Ed is certainly endangering Lou and Richie: first, economically, through his extravagant spending which far exceeds their means, despite his empty reassurances at the dress shop ('Relax, everything's going to be all right'), and, second, less ambiguously, through his overtly murderous designs. But, equally, Lou is putting her own need for financial security ahead of his health: thus, in the middle of Ed's first night home from the hospital, he appears to share Lou's worries to the point of breakdown ('I can't get sick again. What'll happen to you and Richie . . . ?'), though his formulation of this worry as a question suggests a wish for Lou's reply to release him from this burden. But Lou can only take his hand and agree, her face obscured by shadows as she starts to lead him upstairs, her reassurance ('Oh, you'll be all right') as empty and false as his earlier reassurance to her in the course of his spending spree. The film is remarkably symmetrical in its positioning of Ed and Lou as mutually oppressive and oppressed because of circumstances and structures beyond their control. Thus, Lou's jealousy of Pat at the beginning of the film is answered by Ed's later suspicions of Wally; Lou's wearing of the black dress at the bridge party, which makes her stand out as a would-be widow, is echoed by Ed's wearing of a black suit in church, which gives him equal prominence at the point in the film when his plan to murder his family is about to take shape. And, of course, Lou's unconscious desire to see Ed dead is fully reciprocated, as we've seen. There are visual parallels between Ed and Lou as well. For example, Ed sits at his desk enclosed by the angular frame of his lamp as Lou presses him for details of the PTA meeting she and Wally were discussing behind his back, Ed replying sarcastically: 'Oh, so you do remember what you were talking about. Did you make a full report, Wally? I'm sure you did.' And, after Wally has knocked Ed out near the end of the film, the jagged bits of wood from the broken banisters similarly frame Lou as she telephones for an ambulance in the background of the shot.

I argued earlier that Lou's resentments were more overt at first, and Ed's more successfully repressed, but as the film progresses Ed's resentments emerge more and more forcefully, as Lou becomes increasingly surreptitious and deceptive in response. Yet if Ed's initial state of distraction prevented him from paying due attention to the nuances of social life around him, now he doesn't miss a trick (for example, the fact that Lou and Wally *were* discussing him behind his back when he comes home from work early and discovers them together, or Lou's 'hypocritical tone of voice' as she tries to soothe him with false endearments, and so on). His newly acquired clear-sightedness ('I see through you as clearly as I see through this glass pitcher') is not complete, however, and he still tends to read events in terms of un-motivated personal betrayal, blind to the economic underpinnings which determine Lou's behaviour. This is most demonstrably the case – if relatively underplayed by the film – in the scene after church when Lou is about to change her dress and Ed insists in some puzzlement that she keep it on ('First you didn't want to wear it to church . . .'). Her reason for this, though opaque to Ed, is clear enough to the attentive viewer who had earlier noted the promise she made to the dress shop rep-resentative, when he came to call the previous day, that the dress would be returned on Monday if there was any problem with Ed's cheque. Economic determinants –

rather than arbitrary resistance to Ed's wishes – are to blame. Ed's blindness to the broader picture is also emphasised in the mathematical problem he sets Richie:

> *Ed:* A and B are hired to cut wood at fifty cents a cord. Write it down. A can cut a cord in 6 hours, B in 5 hours. Now, think. How long will it take them both to cut a cord?
> *Richie:* Fifty cents a cord . . .
> *Ed:* Richie, don't you see, the fifty cents doesn't make any difference. Leave the fifty cents out and go on from there.

Though Ed is correct in purely mathematical terms, his comment reveals a lack of interest in economics which blinkers him to Lou's omnipresent concerns.

One further instance of Ed's lack of perspective is the way he projects his own limitations onto others whom he then denounces for faults which are his own. Thus, when he accuses the milkman of envying him 'because I work with my mind', the fact that Ed is wearing the green cardigan that he'd worn at the taxi company where he works on the side alerts us to the possibility that 'filled with envy and malice' is a more accurate description of Ed himself. That both the milkman and Richie look to Lou – standing behind Ed and not directly in his line of vision – for cues as to how to react gives further emphasis to our sense of Ed as essentially disempowered and hardly a suitable object of envy. Further, the connotations which accrue to the milk-man in this scene draw on a number of other moments in the film. In contrast to Wally's more manly diet of steaks which, on the evidence of his groceries, seem to constitute his only food, milk is associated not only with Lou's betrayal (when, by giving Richie a glass of milk, she disobeys Ed's order not to let him have his dinner until he's solved the mathematical problem), but with her treatment of both Richie and Ed as children. Thus, she complains when Ed plays football in the house with Richie in an earlier scene that 'You kids are going to wreck something' and, when Ed asks for sandwiches, she replies that he had half the roast at dinner, offering him, instead, a glass of warm milk. In contrast, when Wally concocts the heftier 'tiger's milk' (a mixture of yoghurt and molasses), ostensibly to build Ed up, it is Lou to whom he offers it to taste (telling her it'll 'really put hair on your chest'), since Ed has been kept in hospital for another night. Whether milk is offered to Ed or given away to someone else, whether it functions, that is, as a sign of nurturing or of be-trayal, its symbolic effect is to place Ed in the role of hungry child and Lou in the role of mother.

At the PTA meeting, as noted earlier, Ed belittles 'the unspoiled instincts of child-hood', claiming instead that 'childhood is a congenital disease, and the purpose of education is to cure it'. He dismisses 'emotional security' as 'hogwash', advocating a repressive regime involving work, discipline and duty, but his later comment – 'I'm hungry too' – when Lou begs him to let Richie have his dinner (instead of insisting that he work at the problem Ed has set him), hints at his own need for emotional nourishment. That Ed's anger at Lou is partly the anger of an emotionally needy 'child' directed at his 'mother' is fairly obviously implied – though in a somewhat dis-placed manner – when Ed is asked to look after Pat's class on his first day back from the hospital, and one of her young pupils describes his painting to Ed: 'This is a man. He's just mad at his *mother*.' Later, at the PTA meeting, just after he has referred to the children as 'poor bewildered kids', Ed's head is perfectly framed by one of the paintings on the wall behind him – not the same painting as before, but one which appears similarly dark and emotionally stormy. So Ed is linked not just to the absent-minded dutifulness and compensatory face-saving of the older children in his own class (like Joe), as argued earlier, but to the childish rage of the younger ones as well. Like Shakespeare's Cassius, to whom he refers in his class, Ed too has a lean and hungry look which may be dangerous. His repressive words to the gathered parents, advising them on the need to control and contain the instincts of childhood, are in tension with his implied identification with these angry children and the need for the angry child within him to be heard.

The most obvious example of Ed projecting outward aspects of himself is to be found in his explanation to Lou of the decision to kill their son, surely a description of himself at that point much more than of Richie: 'What future can we reasonably see for him now, growing up into a man who feels himself above the law, above ethics, when we're no longer here to restrain him, watch over him. Who knows what crimes, even murder. . .' If the milkman represents for Ed his own 'littleness' and envy of others, then his vision of Richie grown up is a reflection of his guilty fantasies of no longer occupying his place as a victim of patriarchy, but usurping the place of patriarchy itself ('above the law, above ethics . . .'). Faced with these alternatives, for Richie and for himself, of utter powerlessness, on the one hand, and utter power, on the other – alternatives, in the terms of my argument, of belittlement and monstrous augmentation – murder and suicide present themselves with a certain cogency to Ed as the only solutions. But the film has other plans.

In one sense, Ed does symbolically die. Thus, Lou complains to the doctors who have put him under sedation, 'You've had him like a dead man in there for over thirty hours'. And what he wakes to is a state of permanent childlike dependence upon Lou who has been given life-and-death control over his medication ('This time it'll be in carefully prescribed dosage which you will have to supervise,' she's told by Dr Norton). The 'angry child' within Ed has now been repressed rather than heard, and his hunger will be fed with pills; patriarchy – through its representatives, the doctors – has saved him from himself (just as, at the taxi company, Ed had 'saved' a cab-driver addicted to gambling by taking care not to assign him any runs to the track). Ed's previous identification with the biblical Abraham has given place to a dream of Abraham Lincoln from which he wakes; however, Ed is now not identifying with Lincoln himself, but merely walking by his side like a dutiful son. Though the popular myth of Lincoln is as the liberator of the slaves, the self-proclaimed motive which drove him to war was the preservation of the Union at all costs, and this too is relevant here. The ambiguities of Lincoln as liberator/restorer are matched by Ed's description of him: 'I walked with Lincoln. He was as big and ugly and beautiful as he was in life'. Though Ed now claims to remember everything, with Dr Norton's approval, what he recalls is not his pain and anger, but his guilt. As Dr Norton leaves the room – like Lincoln, restoring the union of Ed, Richie and Lou – he turns off the red light outside the door, red having been associated throughout the film with Ed's pain, anger and disease. Ed has now been 'cured', his legacy of future pain displaced onto Richie through the red jacket his son continues to wear. For, although Richie is unhappy at having to become a man in Ed's terms by playing football, he

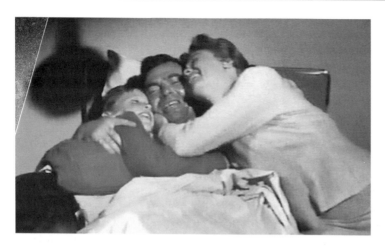

Bigger than Life.
Richie, Ed and Lou
cling together at the
end of the film.

cannot remain a child forever. Ed, however, has become 'arrested' (the term he'd used when describing a state of permanent childhood in his PTA speech), while Lou, though she may now be in control of his destiny, is still as economically disenfranchised as before. All three are prisoners of the larger patriarchal structures which enclose them and determine their futures with such remorseless logic as they cling to one another with apparent relief but more than a little desperation.

Schindler's List

I have described *Schindler's List* as a war film which is broadly melodramatic, though this is not as straightforward as it sounds. Although the film's setting is the Second World War, it is clearly neither a battle film nor a Home Front picture, and has closer affinities with what one might call a Holocaust film or an anti-Nazi film or even, more generally, a film of Jewish persecution, none of which necessarily implies either a war film or the unproblematically melodramatic: consider, for example, *Once upon a Honeymoon*, *The Sound of Music* and *Fiddler on the Roof* (Norman Jewison, 1971). A film's subject matter is far less of a determining factor than one might imagine. I am not primarily concerned with whether 'war film' or 'Holocaust film' is the better generic label, but I do wish to argue for *Schindler's List* as melodramatic in its concentration on the idea of being a man and on the various ways in which this can be achieved in an extremely repressive and hierarchical narrative world.

Before I turn to these matters, it is worth noting that, although it is unthinkable that anyone would presume to describe *Schindler's List* as a comedy, Spielberg is nonetheless audacious in his use of humour, especially in the film's first hour. This seems to me to be an important aspect of the film and needs to be elaborated at some length. For example, when Schindler (Liam Neeson) first appears near the beginning of the film, following the German invasion of Poland in September 1939, we see him preparing to go out – pouring himself a drink, laying out his clothes, getting dressed – in a series of isolated shots of his hands, parts of his body, his Nazi lapel pin and so on, his identity not only fragmented and blatantly constructed, but also a source of mystery to the waiters and Nazi officers in the restaurant where he goes who are intrigued by him and wonder who he is, as he sits smoking a cigarette, his hand partially concealing his face while he observes the scene. By sheer force of personality and a calculated display of hospitality and *bonhomie*, he charms various high-ranking officers and their pretty female companions into joining him at his table (while at the same time subtly distancing himself from them by requesting French, rather than German, wine). Later in the evening, the party around Schindler having grown considerably, he is seen towering above his companions and singing with some robustness in their midst, as the *maître d'*, who had earlier puzzled over Schindler's identity, beams proudly to a newly arrived officer, 'That's Oskar Schindler!' The humour relies largely on our knowing that Schindler is an operator, manipulating the Nazis for his own – as yet undisclosed – ends. He is palpably not one of them, so we can appreciate him as a self-confident charmer, while enjoying their gullibility.

When, in the next scene, Schindler seeks out Itzhak Stern (Ben Kingsley), a Jew, to solicit his help in managing – and finding backers for – the enamelware factory he proposes to set up, Stern is at first seen as a small, background figure in a busy office at the Judenrat headquarters, suggesting an unfragmented but essentially power-less man (in contrast to the initial images of Schindler as fragmented but in control). If the humour in the restaurant scene is at the expense of the too-easily-impressed and status-conscious Germans confronted by Schindler's bountiful conviviality, now Schindler's mastery of presentation itself comes under critical scrutiny through Stern's pointed irony: 'Let me understand. *They* put up all the money, *I* do all the work. What, if you don't mind my asking, would *you* do?' This remark, as well as Schindler's humourless reply that he would provide 'a certain panache', simultaneously confirms our sense of Schindler from the opening scene while relocating us morally with Stern.

Stern's use of humour to clarify his moral position is an important element in Schindler's transformation from self-serving opportunist to hero. A good example of this is when Schindler asks Stern whether the factory is likely to continue to do well:

> *Schindler:* Any reason to think next month will be worse?
> *Stern:* The war could end.

Stern's ironic criticism of Schindler – the implication being that their interests are not yet the same – is different from the humour the film offers us in Schindler's manipulation of the Nazis (and, eventually, of Amon Goeth/Ralph Fiennes in par-ticular) in that Schindler is fully aware of what Stern is up to and, despite his expressions of annoyance, accepts Stern's remarks. Thus, after a one-armed machinist whom Stern has recruited to work in the factory insists on thanking Schindler, later in the same scene, for saving his life, Schindler tells Stern never to embarrass him in that way again:

> *Schindler:* Did you happen to notice that that man had one arm?
> *Stern:* Did he?

What is noteworthy is not just the fact that the implicit humour is shared by the two men at this point, but the way in which, when shortly afterwards the one-armed man is shot by a German soldier while at work shovelling snow, Schindler protests to a high-ranking Nazi acquaintance in a scene intercut with the killing so that we see the blood spreading in the snow as they speak, that the man was a skilled machinist ('He was a metal-press operator – quite skilled'), echoing Stern's disavowal of the fact that the machinist was so obviously ill-suited to his job. What I wish to argue is that Stern in some sense stands in for Schindler as rescuer (by hiring a one-armed man, for example) until Schindler himself is ready to take on this role, using humour to educate him and set an example, and that Schindler increasingly comes to share Stern's position as the film progressively darkens and its humour is drained away. Thus, the structure of the joke quoted earlier ('Any reason to think next month will be worse?' 'The war could end') is taken up and repeated by Schindler when Goeth, the Commandant of Plaszów, admires Schindler's elegant suit.

> *Schindler:* I'd say I'd get you one, but the man who made it is
> probably dead.

However, this remark is much flatter and lacks the ironic humour of the earlier one, while similarly disguising a moral judgment as a statement of fact ('The war could end', '. . . the man . . . is probably dead'). But, unlike Stern's remark to Schindler, Schindler's remark is lost on Goeth.

The strategy of draining humour from the film's narrative world as the war progresses and the horrors proliferate (while nonetheless echoing its earlier jokes in some way to remind us of the loss) applies not just to Stern and his interactions with Schindler, but to the ironic commentary of the film itself on various characters and events. For example, a scene in which Schindler moves into a new apartment whose Jewish occupants have presumably been dispossessed is intercut with one of a Jewish couple being relocated in an already overcrowded flat. Schindler's remark as he inspects his new home – 'It could not be better' – contrasts with their comments as they inspect theirs:

> *Woman:* It could be worse.
> *Man:* How, tell me? How on earth could it *possibly* be *worse?*

At this point, as yet another group of people enter the flat and greet them politely, the film delivers its punchline. Such a device has a long pedigree: one can cite Preston Sturges's more straightforwardly comic use of this structure in *Hail the Conquering Hero* (1944) when a group of fellow Marines escorts a reluctant Woodrow Truesmith (Eddie Bracken) home after he's been discharged from service because of hay-fever, the men having convinced Woodrow's mother that he was wounded in action. When he objects to the pretence, and more particularly to wearing a uniform to which he's no longer entitled, the Sergeant (William Demarest) dismisses his scruples: 'Who's gonna notice anything? You slip off the train, we'll kinda surround you, we slip up a side street, your mother's waiting on the front porch, you put your arms around her, you slip outta uniform . . .' and so on. From this we cut to the huge crowd, band, banners and placards awaiting the train, producing a comic contradiction of the Sergeant's words, as in *Schindler's List*. In Spielberg, however, the moment is repeated with a difference later on, and, as in my other examples, the later echo is both humourless and chilling, as a woman in the Krakow Ghetto in the winter of 1942 tells her friends, 'There is no down from here. This is it. This is the bottom'. Of course, the punchline in this case – though not delivered until later in the film, but fully anticipated by the viewer – is Auschwitz.

44

The conversation in the Krakow Ghetto began with one of the men telling the others how he'd awakened from a dream of being broke and sharing a room with twelve people he didn't know 'only to discover I was broke and sharing a room with twelve people I didn't know.' As he laughs, a woman asks him, 'You laugh at that?' and he replies, 'I have to laugh'. Here, Jewish humour is used in its traditional role as a strategy of self-defence. Indeed, the film as a whole may be deploying such a strategy in its early stages to help the viewer to deal with what is to come. This in no way lessens the horror, but permits us a degree of ironic distance.

Another sort of joke, which occurs twice in the film's first hour, also has the effect of pulling us back from unfolding events. Its success depends on our knowledge that Schindler is an unapologetic womaniser, a fact made clear in the scene where he interviews a series of women to be his secretary, and is attentive to the pretty ones, yet obviously bored by an unattractive older woman who types at great speed. Later on, when his wife Emilie (Caroline Goodall) unexpectedly turns up at his flat only to have the door opened by a half-naked woman (who hurriedly dresses and slips away), Schindler, though somewhat ill at ease, makes no excuses. When Emilie and Oskar leave the building together, the doorman takes Emilie for one of the many young women who visit his flat, and she later agrees to stay on in Krakow only if Schindler promises she'll never be mistaken for anyone else again (i.e. that he'll be faithful). The film cuts to her leaving on the train as he sees her off. The humour seems to derive from a combination of several elements: disruption of our expectation that a sentimental scene of reconciliation is about to occur, admiration (though not, I think, at Emilie's expense) for Schindler's appealing and unrepentant dedication to the pursuit of pleasure, and complicity with Spielberg who lets us fill in the missing details for ourselves.

In a similarly structured scene whose possible consequences are much more serious, Schindler is interrupted, while in bed making love, by the news that Stern has been rounded up for transportation. At the train station, faced with the indifference of two young officials, Schindler promises to see to it that they are in southern Russia by the end of the month, overstating his own importance in a calculated yet fully confident performance. As he walks alongside the train, calling out Stern's name, the two officials – a clerk and a soldier – suddenly enter the frame calling out 'Stern!' as well. The joke, once more, involves a narrative gap – the offscreen change of heart of the two men – as well as our admiration for Schindler's successful bluff at their expense as he rises to the occasion with total self-assurance. A less obvious joke is that the woman with whom Oskar was in bed seems, if I'm not mistaken, to be the same woman who had first caught his eye when he was dining out with Emilie: in this case, their mutual seduction is the missing offscreen event. It is easy to overlook the fact that the scene is not only an example of outrageous bravado (in terms of both jokes), but also the first instance in the film of Schindler deliberately interrupting his own pleasures to save someone else.

In many ways, Schindler begins as the sort of man so many melodramatic pro-tagonists aspire to become. He is tall, imposing and a successful entrepreneur who is both dedicated to a life of pleasure and luxury and respected by those in power. When Goeth speaks in Schindler's defence after he is jailed for kissing a pretty Jewish woman, his words are tinged with escalating envy: 'He likes women. He likes good-looking women. He sees a beautiful woman, he doesn't think . . . He has so many women. They *love* him . . .' Schindler, too, initially sees himself as successful in terms of a highly conventional version of masculinity inherited from the past and based on rivalry with other men, as he proudly tells Emilie how many people he has on his payroll: 'My father, at the height of his success, had fifty. I've got three hundred and fifty.' In contrast to Ed Avery in *Bigger than Life*, he appears to have it all.

By the end of the film, however, Schindler has been divested of all these qualities, his voice breaking, his steps unsteady as he nearly stumbles to the ground, penniless, on the point of tears, stripped of fine clothes, dressed as a Jewish prisoner and about to go on the run. In the last moments of the war, he tells those he's saved that, in the eyes of the world, he is a war profiteer: 'I am a criminal. At midnight you'll be free, and I'll be hunted.' But this downward trajectory in terms of worldly goods and status has, of course, been a journey of moral growth, and the progressive dismantling of his earlier *bon vivant* image, as he identifies his interests more and more with those of the Jews he saves, is his triumph. Stern begins by asking Schindler, 'What, if you don't mind my asking, would *you* do?' Schindler's faltering response, by the end, is that he didn't do enough: 'I could have got more out. I could have got more. I don't know, if I just . . . I could have got more . . .' Schindler, with his self-torment, transcends the lack of awareness – both of self and of the larger context – which typically characterises the melodramatic protagonist. Further, where typical melo-dramatic males end up in defeat, their desires either repressed or frustrated, Schindler comes to see the moral bankruptcy of such aspirations to power, wealth and the pursuit of pleasure, though he shares with such men the fate of having nowhere to go. The fantasies, which melodrama tends to mobilise, of succeeding as a man in traditional terms (or, in the case of domestic melodrama, of at least preserving the appearance of such success) have lost all meaning for Schindler. As he strips himself of power and wealth but also of heroic stature, attributing it to the Jews themselves instead ('Thank *yourselves*. Thank your fearless Stern'), he seems almost willing to take their place ('. . . you'll be free, and I'll be hunted'). It is as though, in a world where power has become so corrupt, the only moral high ground is failure, which Schindler seems at the end to embrace so avidly, the titles informing us of the failed marriage and business ventures still to come.

I have already suggested that Stern is a key figure in setting Schindler on this path of moral growth, and the process continues throughout the film's first half. But while Stern is the first person Schindler saves, Schindler is nevertheless at pains to present this as an act of self-interest, demanding angrily of Stern, 'What if I got here five minutes later, then where would I be?' As the two walk off, they are passed in the opposite direction by men pushing baggage carts. The film's moral concerns are revealed by the decision to abandon Stern and Schindler at this point and to follow the carts of Jewish possessions as these are taken to rooms filled with piles of goods being sorted, including a stack of photographs suggesting a multitude of unknown lives. Seated in a row of Jewish jewellers is a man sorting diamonds. As a pile of teeth is dumped onto the table in front of him, he looks at them, then removes his glasses in silent comprehension of the significance and enormity of these traces of human life.

This sense of the broader picture is more disturbingly presented later in the film when the women and children who are supposed to be sent to Schindler's Brinnlitz factory in his home town are mistakenly routed to Auschwitz and enter the showers, expecting to be killed. However, their panic is misplaced and, after what turns out to be only a shower after all, the women and children, now dressed, walk off to the left as another group of women and children walk to the gas chambers on the right. The moral intricacy of this scene and the complexity of our response are underlined shortly afterwards when Schindler, his eyes in shadow as he pours diamonds on the desk of the officer he's attempting to bribe for the safe return of 'his' Jews, is offered 300 new workers instead, replying with calm deliberation: 'Yes, yes, I understand. I want *these*'. So, far from allowing us to take any easy pleasure in the rescues Schindler effects, the film makes us share his tormented awareness that he can never do enough. All he can do is as much as he can, but the logical conclusion of this is that he must strip himself, finally, of any sign of privilege or difference – including the status of hero itself – which distinguishes him from those he rescues (thus, his distress at having kept his car and Nazi lapel pin which might have purchased a few more lives). He must effectively dissolve his identity in theirs.

The turning point in Schindler's moral growth is his witnessing of the liquidation of the Krakow Ghetto on 13th March 1943, about an hour into the film. This scene is bracketed by our first introduction to Amon Goeth just beforehand, and Schindler's first meeting with him shortly after. Goeth is an interesting example of a melo-dramatic protagonist, whereas Schindler, as we've seen, is more complex. Not only does Goeth aspire to a masculinity of absolute power while remaining blind to the larger forces which shape and constrain him, but the dichotomy between the domestic and an imaginary elsewhere so central to the masculine fantasies called into play by melodramatic films is given particular prominence by his occupying an incongruous domestic space in the middle of Plaszów. When he asks where he'll be living and is shown the villa overlooking the camp, he complains, 'That's not a villa . . . it's a house'; and when he chooses a maid from a row of female prisoners, he asks, 'Which of you has . . . um . . . domestic experience?' Yet, just as Schindler's choice of secretary was based on good looks rather than skills and experience, Goeth chooses Helen Hirsch (Embeth Davidtz), the one woman who has not raised her hand, having suddenly decided that he doesn't want someone else's maid after all. But whereas Schindler is open and unapologetic about the delight he takes in pretty women, Goeth has chosen a woman for whom he can never admit his desire.

Schindler's List.
The first meeting between Amon Goeth (Ralph Fiennes) and Helen Hirsch (Embeth Davidtz).

Schindler's List. The woman engineer argues with Goeth and is shot on his orders. Helen witnesses the woman's death as Goeth leaves.

That Goeth's attraction to Helen and simultaneous inability to acknowledge his desire are at the heart of his domestic arrangements is indicated in part by Helen's location in the basement of the villa in two crucial scenes involving Schindler and Goeth respectively (and to which we shall return), a location which presents Helen – and the ambivalent feelings she arouses in Goeth – as his guilty secret, the scandal of which must be hidden at all costs. Goeth's sudden interest in Helen is interrupted by the hurried approach of another young woman prisoner, an engineer, who protests that the foundations of a building being put up under her supervision in the camp are inadequate and are bound to subside and then collapse. Goeth's brutal reply to an accompanying guard – 'Shoot her' – with Helen standing by as a silent witness is testimony to the strength of the repressiveness needed to quiet his newly awakened feelings for Helen as he displaces them onto her more vocal and argumentative surrogate whom he kills, convincing himself that he has done his duty, while keeping Helen herself alive.

The next sequence in the film, in which the Krakow Ghetto is liquidated, is introduced by Goeth speaking to his men: 'For six centuries there has been a Jewish Krakow. Think about that. By this evening those six centuries are a rumour. They never happened. Today is history.' The film cuts from the grandiose self-importance of Goeth's words to Schindler and a woman friend riding on horseback above the town, accidental witnesses to the events below which, again, as with the earlier rescue of Stern at the station, operate as an interruption to Schindler's pleasures, just as the sequence marks a definitive end to the pleasure we took in some of the humorous moments cited earlier. The sequence lasts about a quarter of an hour and is the first sustained assault on the viewer's sensibilities (previously we'd seen a few arbitrary shootings, but little more): it is almost unbearable to watch. The editing is extremely complex, with a multitude of separate mini-narratives following in rapid succession, various threads being picked up again as the sequence goes on. Amongst many other Jews, some of the *Schindlerjuden* appear at various points in the sequence, though their special status within the narrative is not yet signalled.

Both Schindler and his friend are clearly moved by what they see – a gratifying indication that his choice in women is not wholly determined by their looks, as we may have too hastily assumed. The sequence overall, though crucial in setting Schindler on the path of his first disinterested rescues, does not exclusively privilege his viewpoint. We see many events which Schindler and his companion could not possibly have witnessed, and the Jews themselves are portrayed not simply as helpless victims, but as individuals characterised by numerous instances of courage, resourcefulness,

and, as far as possible, resistance (as with the doctor and nurse who give their patients a merciful death). However, despite our more privileged viewpoint, we share with Schindler the horror not just of what has unfolded before our eyes but, in contrast to the resourcefulness of the Jews within the sequence, of our utter passivity in the face of it. From now on, Schindler will take action, and our pleasure will derive almost entirely from this development and the decency it reveals.

At this stage in Schindler's development, Stern, who is now a prisoner in Plaszów, continues to function as his guide, telling him of worthy fellow prisoners in danger through having attracted the attention of the Commandant. One of them is Levartov (Ezra Dagan), a rabbi turned hingemaker whose day's output Goeth finds too small during his inspection of the camp's metalworks factory. When Goeth takes him outside to shoot him, ignoring Levartov's explanation that he was shovelling coal all morning while the machines were being recalibrated, his gun repeatedly misfires and he settles for hitting Levartov on the head. When Schindler hears Stern's story, he casually hands Stern his lighter to use as a bribe to get Levartov put on a list of workers assigned to Schindler's factory, the apparent indifference of his manner belied by the moral commitment that his act discloses.

Our pleasure, after the earlier helplessness of witnessing the liquidation of the ghetto, is intense, and it is further reinforced by a second rescue soon afterwards. Following Goeth's summary execution of a man randomly chosen from an assembled group, none of whom will admit to the theft of a chicken, a young boy displays quick thinking and the same resourcefulness we've already seen in the Krakow Ghetto by catching Goeth's attention, pointing at the executed man and identifying him as the thief. Once again, Stern is instrumental in the boy's rescue, playing a verbal game with Schindler the rules of which are clear to them both:

> *Stern:* He's very gifted.
> *Schindler:* Yeah, sure, bring him over.

as Schindler hands his cigarette case to Stern. The fastidiousness with which Stern and Schindler play their parts – Stern being careful to make a special case for the boy, as if it is 'just this once', and Schindler pretending casual indifference – disguise their growing mutual trust and respect and their recognition of the very high stakes involved. Both are well aware that there is an endless stream of people in need of rescue and that the lighter and cigarette case are only the first of Schindler's possessions and pleasures which he will be required to give up as he reconstitutes his identity in less materialistic terms through his growing commitment to others.

Schindler's List.
'. . . he won't even let
you wear the star.'
Schindler (Liam
Neeson) to Helen.

When a young woman, Regina Perlman (Bettina Kupfer), who has been passing as Gentile in the world outside the camp, comes to plead with Schindler for her parents inside (having had to put on make-up and more becoming clothes before he would agree to see her), his response reflects his anger at his growing reputation as a good man.

> *Regina:* They say that no one dies here. They say your factory is a
> haven. They say you are good.
> *Schindler:* Who says that?
> *Regina:* Everyone.

When he tells her she's been misled and threatens her with arrest, Regina runs out, and Schindler later berates Stern for expecting him to save everyone, stressing the personal danger to himself. No longer welcoming the war as an opportunity, as he had when discussing his business affairs with his wife, he now speaks more pensively of Goeth and how war always brings out the worst in people, 'never the good, always the bad, *always* the bad'. Had the war not happened, Goeth's good side alone would show, his love of good food, good wine, and women (and 'killing', Stern adds). The irony, of course, is that, in Schindler's case, the war is bringing out what Stern will later describe as 'an absolute good' and that the love of food, wine and women which characterises Schindler as much as it does Goeth is precisely what he must give up to achieve this. When Schindler asks Stern with some impatience what he expects him to do, Stern hastily replies, 'Nothing, nothing . . .', and the scene ends with Schindler handing over his watch to get the Perlmans out as their daughter had asked. Schindler is now acting without being prompted by Stern, and, as we see the couple enter Schindler's factory in long shot, we share the satisfaction of their daughter, who is placed, smiling, in the foreground of the frame, though not the satisfaction of Schindler himself. The motive for Schindler's righteous acts is never the pleasure that they will give him; on the contrary, the sacrifice of pleasure and self-satisfaction is one of their inevitable results, as his token resistance makes clear. It is merely that, as a decent man, he no longer has a choice.

We cut from the Perlmans' daughter to an exterior shot of Goeth's villa, and then to Helen Hirsch in the cellar as Schindler comes down to get some wine. His words of reassurance to Helen ('I'm Schindler') indicate that his reluctance to acknowledge the Perlman girl's remarks ('They say no one dies here . . . They say you are good') in the earlier scene was prudent rather than self-deceiving. Oskar and Helen talk quietly as she confides her fears of being shot, and he comforts her that Goeth 'won't shoot you because he enjoys you too much. He enjoys you so much he won't even let you wear the star. He doesn't want anyone else to know it's a Jew he's enjoying.' Later, when Schindler rejoins Goeth on the balcony, he tries to convince the drunken Commandant of the supreme power of pardoning those one believes one has every reason to kill. The novelty of this idea leads Goeth to try it out a few times: 'Go ahead, go on, leave, leave. I pardon you,' he tells Lisiek (Wojciech Klata), the boy who is cleaning his bath but has failed to remove all the stains. However, when he then looks at himself in the bathroom mirror and says 'I pardon you' to his own reflection, he is strangely disturbed, examines his fingernails, returns to the balcony

Schindler's List. Schindler convinces Goeth of the power of pardoning. Goeth's response. Cleaning the bath. Goeth pardons Lisiek (Wojciech Klata) for failing to remove the stains. Goeth pardons himself, and notices that he needs a manicure.

Schindler's List. Lisiek is killed by Goeth.
The manicure.

and arbitrarily starts shooting once again, killing Lisiek, who is now walking below him outside. Stern walks by the boy's body, then the film cuts to Goeth's hand as Helen gives him a manicure, the atmosphere charged with (her) unspoken fears and (his) desires. The fact that he looks at his fingernails between 'pardoning' himself and resuming the killing suggests that thinking about his need to be pardoned has given rise to thoughts of Helen (at any rate, to the extent of noticing that he needs a manicure), and that the resurgence of this desire for (at least) a manicure in turn calls up a repressive need to kill another Jew. This is perhaps not a random killing after all: not only does the boy's job, cleaning the bath, suggest a subliminal link with Helen, who is after all Goeth's maid, but his inability to clean away the stains suggests a thematic link with Goeth himself, who cannot cleanse himself of his 'impure' desires. The killing is a repetition of the displaced attempt to disavow his desire for Helen in the earlier shooting of the woman engineer, her complaint about faulty foundations in danger of collapse also of possible symbolic relevance to Goeth. While the measure of Schindler's transformation can be seen in the contrast between his opportunistically constructed identity in the opening scene ('That's Oskar Schindler!') and his quiet acknowledgement of the man he's now become in the scene with Helen ('I'm Schindler'), Goeth is unable to change, trapped as he is in the hell of his own contradictions.

Goeth's contradictory desires are most clearly manifest in the scene which parallels Schindler's visit to Helen in the cellar: Goeth, too, visits her there and, in an extraordinary excess of self-deception, offers her a reference for use after the war. This scene is complexly intercut with three others: a Jewish wedding inside the camp; Schindler applauding a woman singer in a club; then Schindler kissing a series of women at a party at his factory – evidently somewhat later – where Goeth and Stern are toasting him in honour of his birthday, ending with Schindler kissing a

Jewish girl and young woman who present him with his cake on behalf of all the workers. In the scene with Goeth and Helen, fragmented by its intercutting with these three other scenes, Goeth's conflicting feelings pour out unrestrained. One moment, he tells Helen he wants to 'reach out and touch you in your loneliness' and wonders what it would be like, musing, 'Hath not a Jew eyes?' as he touches her hair; the next moment, on the verge of kissing her, he shifts to brusque denial – 'No, I don't think so' – and blames the silent Helen for having nearly talked him into it. His violence escalates, as in earlier scenes, in proportion to the strength he must exert to repress his desires, and from Goeth slapping Helen, we cut to Schindler clapping, to the bride and groom kissing, to Helen cowering, to Schindler blowing a kiss to the singer, to Goeth throwing Helen down . . . slapping her again . . . knocking over shelves, as the interwoven scenes of the newly married couple and of Schindler kissing numerous women provide a mocking counterpoint to Goeth's confusion.

When we next see Goeth, he is undergoing a medical examination on his balcony, as he tells his girlfriend of the latest selection process following the arrival of a shipment of Hungarian Jews: 'They're going to separate the sick from the healthy, to make room.' The irony of his own medical examination occurring at this point is compounded by the fact that his own 'sickness' (which we have so recently witnessed) remains undiagnosed. The depiction of the selection, about two hours into the film, is reminiscent of the liquidation of the ghetto an hour earlier: in the broad sweep of its events, in the resourcefulness of the Jewish women who prick their fingers, smearing the blood on their cheeks to give the appearance of health, and in the new depths of horror to which the audience is subjected, especially when the relief of the smiling women who have escaped selection is shattered by the sight of truckloads of their waving children being driven past (though a few have managed to hide).

As the prisoners selected to be killed are loaded onto trains, Schindler arrives stylishly dressed in a white suit and hat. He basks in the sunshine ('Oh, another beautiful day') and fans himself with his hat; a water tap is prominently positioned in the foreground of one shot. It is all, of course, a meticulously constructed performance on his part, and Schindler's real purpose becomes clear when he turns to Goeth and suggests casually, 'What do you say we get your fire hoses out here and hose down the cars . . . [Here he laughs in apparent self-mockery] . . . Indulge me.' Schindler is astute in addressing his request to Goeth in terms of the provision of a pleasure ('Indulge me'), for it is Schindler's jocularity and apparent dedication to the pursuit of pleasure which continue to convince Goeth that – despite Oskar's evident eccentricities – he is still indisputably 'one of us'. As the sequence unfolds, Schindler's mask of unconcern begins to slip, as he insists on more water and asks for longer hoses to reach the more distant carriages. We see Stern, and then Goeth, watching Schindler's increasingly earnest and purposeful behaviour, his jacket and hat now removed as he paces impatiently up and down the platform overseeing the process. The sequence ends with a close shot of Goeth, his expression serious.

The tactic whereby Schindler, although sacrificing his life of pleasure to his single-minded attempt to save as many lives as he can, must nevertheless continue to present the façade of the companionable *bon vivant*, is more and more difficult to sustain, and his dealings with Goeth (as the selection scene has already shown) become progressively more pragmatic and less disguised. Goeth is, perhaps, a bit slower to acknowledge this than Schindler is to drop his pretences, and his comment, in the hellish scene where thousands of Jewish corpses are exhumed and thrown into burning pits in April 1944 – 'The party's over, Oskar' – implies an illusion of shared regret rather than any awareness that Oskar has long since abandoned the role of willing party-goer at Amon's feast.

As more and more Jews are being transported to Auschwitz, Schindler converts his assets into cash and asks Goeth to let him take 'his' workers to his Brinnlitz factory:

> *Schindler:* Look, all you have to do is tell me what it's worth to you.
> What's a person worth...?
> *Goeth:* No, no, no, no. What's one worth to *you*?

The cold pragmatism of Schindler's haggling with Goeth is replaced in the following scene by Schindler's concentrated struggle to remember as many names as possible to include on his list, pushing Stern, as he types, to come up with additional names as well ('More, more . . .'). When it suddenly dawns on Stern that Schindler is paying for each name, Schindler is once again jokingly self-dismissive: 'If you are still working for me, I'd expect you to talk me out of it. It's costing me a fortune.' The resumption of humour at this point in the film – however self-deprecating – is the first indication that the worst of the horrors may be over, although Schindler's journey to the very doors of death at Auschwitz, when the women and children are sent there by mistake, is yet to come; they will, however, return in safety.

Leaving a single blank space at the bottom of his list, Schindler approaches Goeth one last time and asks for Helen Hirsch to be included, offering to gamble with Amon for her life, since, otherwise, she will surely end up in Auschwitz.

> *Goeth:* She's not going to Auschwitz. I'd never do that to her. No, I want her to . . . um . . . come back to Vienna with me, I want her to come . . . come work for me there. I want to . . . uh . . . grow old with her.
> *Schindler:* Are you mad? Amon, you can't take her to Vienna with you.
> *Goeth:* No, of course I can't. It's what I'd *like* to do . . .

Now that all pretence has been dropped between them, Goeth can openly admit to Schindler his desire for a life with Helen, but he is far too complicit by now with the forces of repression for this to be more than a crazy fantasy. The next scene, in which the *Schindlerjuden* give their names and are checked off on the list, ending with Helen Hirsch, is another repetition of the humorous technique used twice in the first hour of the film whereby we are shown the consequence of a process which has taken place offscreen (Oskar refusing to be faithful to his wife; the officials at the station deciding it is prudent to get Stern off the train; and, here, Schindler 'winning' Helen in a card game with Goeth). Helen's rescue is no joke, but the repetition of this structure combined with the happy outcome of the offscreen event continue the process of reassurance – notwithstanding its bitter disruption by the shower scene at Auschwitz – embodied in the film's final scenes.

Yet the guarded optimism which this may be taken to imply is heavily qualified. It is true that the film's earlier strategy of echoing humorous moments with non-humorous ones of similar structure has in one or two instances been reversed, for example, in the resumption of a gently ironic humour between Schindler and Stern, as mentioned earlier, and in the way that the near-tragic episode of Goeth's pistol repeatedly misfiring as he tries to shoot Levartov is turned into a 'joke' at Goeth's expense in the scene when he's hanged at the end of the war and it takes several bungled attempts to kick over the stool on which he's standing before the execution is successfully accomplished. But both these examples – especially Goeth's death – have such dark undertones that to call them instances of humour is to overstate the case. The difficulties of reintroducing humour in the aftermath of Auschwitz are reflected in the bitterness which qualifies our satisfaction at Goeth suffering such a pathetically bungled and ignominious death.

If humour must be reinvented, then so too must language, and Stern's brave attempts at irony make this clear when, believing his transportation to Auschwitz to be imminent in the later stages of the war, he is assured by Schindler that Goeth has given his word that Stern will receive special treatment in the camp.

> *Stern:* The directives coming in from Berlin mention special treatment
> more and more often. I'd like to think that's not what you mean.
> *Schindler:* Preferential treatment, all right? Do we have to invent a
> whole new language?
> *Stern:* I think so.

Schindler goes on to say that all this will be over one day, adding, 'I was going to say we'll have a drink then,' to which Stern replies, 'I think I'd better have it now.' There is sweetness in the depth of their shared understanding that the future is bleak (shared, because Schindler needs no reminder from Stern, having chosen his words with great care: he was 'going to say', but knew better). Their realism contrasts sharply with Goeth's deluded fantasies about growing old with Helen Hirsch.

Not only have humour and language lost their innocence – if they ever had it to begin with – but the world's appearances themselves have become irretrievably blemished and corrupted: the prelude to the scenes of exhumation and cremation already discussed is the sight of children playing innocently in the snow . . . until Schindler inspects the 'snow' on a parked car, gathering it in his palms and rubbing the flakes with his fingers, and realises – as we do – that they are human ash. But if the world's aspect has changed in many ways, one thing remains unaltered. When one of the liberated *Schindlerjuden* asks a Russian soldier where they should go, his reply – 'Don't go east, that's for sure. They hate you there. I wouldn't go west either, if I were you' –

Schindler's List. Children playing as ash falls. Human ash on Schindler's hands.

provides a pessimistic preamble to the scene of Goeth's hanging immediately afterwards, giving an open-endedness to our sense of a just and final retribution, as well as a dashing of hopes about what post-war Europe holds in store. The film ends (as a written title informs us) with 'the Schindler Jews today' presented as a group of people on the horizon who approach us as the film's black-and-white images are replaced by colour. We cut to Schindler's grave, where the survivors, side by side with the actors who played them, place stones around the perimeter of the grave, and the final titles tell us that 'There are fewer than four thousand Jews left alive in Poland today. There are more than six thousand descendants of the Schindler Jews.' So the film is both completely uncynical in its praise of decency while simultaneously pessimistic about the possibilities open to decent men like Schindler in a repressive world which is seen to extend beyond the end of the Second World War and Hitler's defeat. It also extends beyond the narrative frame of the film, as the juxtaposition of actors with their real-life counterparts makes clear. This is our world, and we carry it with us when we leave the cinema.

As with Ed Avery in *Bigger than Life*, who eventually comes to see his death as the only way out of his predicaments, so too, in the case of Schindler, are worldly failure and death the only imaginable outcomes. But, whereas Ed Avery moves between seeing his material failures and lack of power as personal shortcomings, on the one hand, and as regrettable oversights on the part of an ungrateful world, on the other, so that his death can be construed as a noble suicide, Schindler, in contrast, sees wealth and power as rewards for 'good' behaviour in a corrupt world which he increasingly disowns, identifying more and more, as I've argued, with the Jews he saves. Although he is introduced to the path of righteousness by Stern, who initially functions as his conscience, his single-mindedness finally exceeds that of Stern himself, who ends up attempting to become Schindler's consolation instead – though to little effect – insisting that Schindler has done as much as he could ('Oskar, there are eleven hundred people who are alive because of you. Look at them'). Schindler's commitment is absolute, and he follows its implications through to the last detail, even to the extent of deliberately miscalibrating the machines in his Brinnlitz factory so that they will produce faulty shells. When Stern speaks of the danger to them all of sabotaging production in this way (in a reversal of Schindler's concerns in the early stages of the film, when he tells Stern that his attempt to involve Schindler in his rescues is 'dangerous. It's dangerous to *me* . . .'), Schindler replies that they can buy shells from other sources and pass them off as their own.

When the war is on the verge of ending, Schindler invites the guards into the factory itself and takes a final gamble, instructing them that they can kill all the prisoners, as they've been ordered, 'or you could leave and return to your families as men, instead of murderers,' which is what they do. In contrast, Schindler's own homecoming to Brinnlitz is short-lived, as he and his wife must now prepare to flee. Awkwardly, Schindler expresses to Stern his continuing tormented awareness of the lives he couldn't save. A few minutes later, Stern catches him as he stumbles and holds him in his arms, as others surround them and join in the embrace. Like the Jews he's saved and whom he's now forced to leave, Oskar is left to wander in a world that has no use for either them or him.

MEN AND MELODRAMA

My account of *Schindler's List* ends with a description of Oskar Schindler as a wanderer, recalling the character of Ethan Edwards (played by John Wayne) in John Ford's film, *The Searchers* (1956). However, despite the fact that both Oskar and Ethan end up unanchored in the conventional social worlds of their respective films, Ethan's uneasily suppressed desire for a woman he can never have makes him more like Goeth than Schindler, and renders him a deeply troubled and excessively violent melodramatic protagonist (rather than an unproblematic hero). In contrast, Wayne's roles in many other films present him as a more straightforwardly heroic figure, who, like Schindler, is dedicated to defending the safety of those under his protection. Although in almost all his films Wayne's characters are uneasy when placed within a conventional domestic setting and conventional family life, he is nonetheless often a benevolent father figure when he is able to edge the 'mother' out of the picture. In *The Searchers*, however, Ethan is not protective but destructive, at least until the final moments, denying his psychological kinship with the Indians by hating them and all things Indian, both outside and within himself, just as Goeth hates all things Jewish.

Ethan and Goeth are not comparable in all respects, however, since Martha (Dorothy Jordan) – whom Ethan loves but who is married to his brother – is not an Indian, whereas Helen is a Jew. So whereas Ethan can split his ambivalence towards Martha (both desiring her and disavowing this desire) by directing his negative feelings towards the Indian chief, Scar (Henry Brandon), who becomes the focus of his hatred once Martha has been raped and killed, Goeth must first 'remove' Helen's Jewishness ('. . . he won't even let you wear the star') in order that he can direct his hatred onto other Jews while keeping Helen alive as the object of his (repudiated) desire, though her Jewishness breaks through for him in the scene in the cellar when his desire pushes too near to conscious enactment, and he turns his violence on her.

I am aware that my reading of *The Searchers* goes somewhat against the grain of other readings which see Ethan's hatred of the Indians, and of Scar in particular, as a hatred of himself (or of that aspect of himself which would have raped Martha), while Scar's rape of Martha is seen as a playing out of Ethan's repressed desires. I am suggesting that Ethan's hatred is at the same time a hatred of Martha, as, indeed, the violence of his imaginary rape and murder of her (via Scar) makes clear, or at least a hatred of the aspect of Martha which has aroused his desire, as is so clearly the case with Goeth and Helen. In fact, what emerges is a hatred of desire itself, at least when it threatens to bring some sort of male diminishment in its wake (such as Ethan's domestication and spatial confinement had he married Martha in the past, or Goeth's reducing of himself to the point of imprisonment or worse if he were to love a Jew). Melodrama's world is a repressive one inhospitable to the expression of mutual erotic desire. It seems to me to be an absolutely crucial distinction between the melodramatic and the comedic (and an important aspect of their respective interactions with the romantic, as we shall see in Chapter Four) that erotic desire is consistently blocked – or converted to sadistic violence – in the former and given at least the possibility of free play in the latter. Of course, this is not to say that melodrama endorses such blockage whereas comedy condemns it, but rather that, without determining a judgment either way, the melodramatic narrative world says, 'This is how it is' (in terms, that is, of the blockage of desire within its hierarchically structured social domain) where the comedic world says, 'This is how it might be different'.

It is self-evident that the desires of the heterosexual melodramatic male are aroused by those who are different from himself in important respects (most obviously women, but sometimes women who are also marked by racial, ethnic or class differences). Insofar as romantic love is seen to produce a growing mutual identification between lovers which threatens to dissolve their differences, its presence is a troubling disturbance to the hierarchies of difference which underpin the melodramatic world. When men give in to desire (for example, by marrying), this often appears to destabilise the balance of power which melodrama presents as the norm, producing men who feel disempowered at the hands of their wives or lovers, despite the fact that these women remain relatively powerless in the world beyond the home or relationship. Desire between men and women in the melodramatic world is hopelessly enmeshed in these shifting patterns of power, their desirability being the one card women have to play.

So melodramatic films seem to be concerned centrally with confrontations between white mainstream males and a variety of antagonistic others – Indians, Jews, transgressive women and so on – whose otherness accomplishes two related purposes. Firstly, it demonstrates that the melodramatic world is a rigidly hierarchical one where one's difference from other people guarantees either privilege or subordination. Secondly, it provides the possibility of splitting off (and denying or destroying) the desiring aspect of oneself or the desirable aspect of the object of one's passion (by providing a place to project it outward) which, if they were to be accepted as part of the self or of an alluring 'other', would cause this hierarchy based on difference to tumble down. So the repression of desire is necessary to the maintenance of melodrama's narrative world.

Thus, in some genres where categories of difference other than that of gender are readily to hand, the melodramatic male's disavowal of desire can be transformed into a hatred of Indians, Jews, black people, and so on, while a woman bearing none of these additional aspects of otherness can be seen as simultaneously purified of her desirability and of any resultant hatefulness; leaving the male able to love her chastely, purged of any openly acknowledged feelings of desire (as with Martha in *The Searchers* or Helen Hirsch in *Schindler's List*, at least once Helen's Jewishness has been removed in Goeth's imagination). In *film noir*, too, the aggression towards the small-town wife can be deflected onto a *femme fatale* whose infidelities and other transgressions appear to justify the transformation of the male protagonist's sexual desire into violence and revenge. But where such alternative others (alternative to 'respectable' women, that is) are lacking – notably in domestic small-town melodramas – the melodramatic male has two possibilities. He can himself become a monstrous other and an object of self-hatred (as in *The Incredible Shrinking Man* until the spider appears as an alternative object of hate, or in *Bigger than Life* when Ed Avery is cured of his murderous desires but left with his guilt). Or, where sexual desire has proved too strong to be repressed and has led to involvement with a desirable woman (though, if they've been married for some time, the wife's desirability may now be seen as a thing of the past), his anger at his consequent diminishment may be directed at the woman herself (as with Ed Avery while he is still suffering from his drug-induced delusions of grandeur), because there is no opportunity for it to be deflected elsewhere. The marital partnership in particular, which links together the interests of husband and wife – a result negotiated through romance – may decrease the difference in power and standing between them, both within the home and in public perceptions which take them to be presenting a united front.

The search for an elsewhere in melodramatic films must be understood, I think, as an imagined escape from domestic disempowerment whereby the white male, through an aggressive confrontation with those different from himself, can regain the ground he's lost or is in danger of losing in the domestic domain. In this sense, Scott Carey's killing of the spider in the basement (the elsewhere to the world upstairs), Ethan's pursuit of Scar in the wilderness beyond the homesteads, and Goeth's murders of Jews in the camp surrounding his house are displaced assertions of difference from women who are seen to entice them to surrender to sexual desire and relinquish their privileged positions. Because of his location within the world of domestic small-town melodrama, Ed Avery's fantasised elsewhere is less a place apart than an imaginary transformation of himself to a position of power within the home, with his aggression openly aimed at his family. But, as I hinted earlier, the instances of aggression towards the spider, towards Scar, and towards the Jewish population of Plaszów in some sense also represent such hatred towards a woman who was – or continues to be – desired. The fantasies of diminishment and augmentation which characterise the domestic space give way to fantasies of toughness and violence in the space elsewhere.

Emotional blockage – the refusal of the entanglements of sexual desire which typically characterises melodramatic men (regardless of specific genre) – goes hand in hand with a limited range of ways of being a man, toughness and respectability providing the two main models. As I've argued in an article on the psychodynamics of *film noir*'s men ('Psychoanalysis and film noir' in Ian Cameron (ed.), *The Movie Book of Film Noir*, Studio Vista, 1992), toughness and respectability are two versions of the same thing: a solidity which defends the male body against the free flow of desire. The only forms of release from this – at least within melodramatic films – are dissolution and death. Fantasies of augmentation are part of the same defensive dynamic, but whereas the tough men in Westerns, war films and *film noir* tend to be genuinely tough, the augmentation of Ed Avery (to give one example) is only an illusion. Such fantasies of augmentation (and fears of diminishment) are more likely to crop up in domestic melodramas (and domestic settings within other genres), rather than in genres where toughness – as opposed to respectability – is the favoured model, because augmentation suggests a façade or appearance of power, rather than its reality, and suits men disempowered by domesticity who try to save face while in fear of a scandalous revelation of their true dimensions.

Throughout melodramatic films, the blockage of sexual desire gives rise to alternative male appetites – for such things as violence or food, for example, as we've seen. In contrast, Schindler's need to save as many lives as he can (telling Stern, 'More, more . . .' as they compile the life-saving list) is not a matter of appetite and pleasure but of moral urgency. As I've argued earlier in my account of *Schindler's List*, Schindler transcends the position of a melodramatic male by progressively distancing himself from an economy of pleasure involving the processes of repression, displacement and transformation which I've suggested are at work within so many melodramatic films. This is partly possible because, having enjoyed an excess of pleasure up until then and having stepped outside the bounds of a conventional domestic relationship with his wife to do so, he is able to detach himself from the regime of pleasure with much less sense of frustration and unmet needs than might otherwise be the case. He has already achieved the ambitions of the melodramatic male by leaving home and marriage to make his fortune and outperform his father: the realisation of an exemplary version of what I've referred to as a fantasy of augmentation. But, in addition, there is no special woman whose erotic hold on Schindler threatens to diminish him in any way. He moves from one to another with ease and equal delight, and his return to Emilie at the end is not in pursuit of pleasure but is part of his determination to give it up in order to devote himself – now, with Emilie's help – to the protection of 'his' Jews. This is similar to those of John Wayne's heroic characters whose protectiveness is uncomplicated by a sense of repressed desire, though Wayne is often presented more melodramatically in films where his character has an estranged wife, for example, to whom he continues to be strongly attracted. But it is, above all, in Schindler's conscious and willing identi-fication with the Jews that he transcends melodrama most completely, unlike Goeth, who continually seeks to assert his separateness from the Jews through his violent attacks upon them. Schindler not only removes himself from a regime of pleasure, but voluntarily relinquishes his position within a hierarchy of privilege as well.

Before I move on to a consideration of comedy and romance in Chapters Three and Four, a few words need to be said about point of view. I began by suggesting that male and female fantasies of empowerment, disempowerment, revenge and so forth are complementary, so that Ed Avery's fantasy of augmentation, if the film were to be constructed from the point of view of his wife Lou, would have less prominence than the corresponding fantasy of disempowerment on her part. To some extent, *Bigger than Life* does give space to a female point of view, at least more so than *The Incredible Shrinking Man*, where the point of view of Scott Carey's wife is barely acknowledged. Similarly, Lou Avery's fantasies about taking revenge on her husband offer a complement to his fears of diminishment at her hands. Clearly some films are more suppressive of such double – or even multiple – viewpoints than others. I have concentrated more on male than female fantasies both because the vast majority of broadly melodramatic films are centred upon men and because the possibilities open to women within the melodramatic narrative world are more limited, given their more lowly position within its hierarchies of power. It seems that female fantasies are less likely to result in action (however displaced) or to determine the direction of narrative events except indirectly, by provoking a reaction from a male. Thus, whereas Ed Avery actually almost murders his family, his wife Lou merely pauses suggestively on the threshold of the bedroom while her husband falls down ill. She merely 'thinks' him dead, whereas melodramatic males more often seem to act for themselves or, at least, to find a surrogate male to perform such actions on their behalf (as with Ethan and Scar). It would be interesting to test this further by examining melodramas focused specifically on a female point of view. I argued earlier, however, that comedy shows us how the world might be different and that romance is the female's trump card in upsetting traditional relations of power between the sexes. Perhaps comedic and romantic films give a greater prominence to female points of view than most melodramatic films seem to allow.

CHAPTER THREE

COMEDIC MASCULINITIES

COMEDIES OF REGRESSION

I emphasised in Chapter One that I would be largely bypassing genres in this book, preferring to concentrate on the relationship between individual films and much broader concerns. Thus, the three sections of the present chapter discuss various comedic strategies which provide contrasts with the repressiveness of melodramatic films, rather than dealing with particular comic genres. These strategies seem to offer ways of subverting or avoiding melodramatic hierarchies based upon difference and differential power. Where melodramatic men, as we saw in Chapter Two, appear to be threatened by the prospect of surrendering to sexual desire and the domesticity it may entail because of the way such domestic containment diminishes their stature and undermines their privileged status, comedic males – in contrast – are much more positively served when they are toppled from such heights. It is worth looking closely at various comedic strategies which separate male characters from the position they occupy as white adult men within such hierarchical structures: comedic regression, comedic heroism and more flexible forms of romance all provide male characters with new sources and definitions of dignity and sustenance that are lacking or discredited in melodramatic films.

In examining what I have labelled a strategy of regression, my starting point is a Howard Hawks film, *Monkey Business*, chosen both because Hawks's films have often been discussed in terms of male regression and because the film offers remarkably close parallels with the themes and events of its melodramatic counterpart, *Bigger than Life* (which was considered in Chapter Two). Thus, the differences between a clear-cut melodramatic film and a clear-cut comedic one will be thrown into relief by striking similarities of plot and thematic concerns. Both films focus on an absent-minded married man – in *Monkey Business*, Barnaby Fulton, played by Cary Grant – who, though apparently docile in what is revealed to be a marriage where sex plays little part, undergoes an unexpected transformation after taking a (supposedly beneficial) drug. In both cases, suppressed resentments and jealousies come out under the influence of the drug, whose dosage and consequences escalate as the film progresses, and both men come to realise – or are made to do so by others – that it offers no miracles, but must be strictly controlled or even destroyed. Finally, both films end with the married couple reconciled and caught in an embrace, their mutual resentments firmly tucked away. As Victor Perkins puts it, in his article on the comedies of Howard Hawks, *Bigger than Life* 'is virtually a remake of Hawks's picture' ('Comedies,' in *Movie* No. 5, December 1962, p.22). And yet it hardly needs saying that for anyone who has seen both films, the differences between them are significant too: the Avery family have a son, while the Fultons are childless; Ed is the

Monkey Business.
'Not yet, Cary.'

only character in *Bigger than Life* to take the drug and thus isolated in his experience and at the mercy of a number of other people who control him, whereas many of the characters in *Monkey Business* – most crucially, Edwina Fulton (Ginger Rogers), Barnaby's wife – take the rejuvenating drug as well as Barnaby himself; and while the cortisone taken by Ed produces fantasies of augmentation, the formula that Barnaby and Edwina take makes them regress psychologically to a childlike state. Most importantly, however, the world of *Bigger than Life* is a dangerous one, while that of *Monkey Business* is safe.

Monkey Business begins with a shot of Cary Grant opening the front door of his character's house, followed by a voice on the soundtrack which one presumes to be that of Hawks saying, 'Not yet, Cary', followed by a repetition of the same sequence of events. By the time of Grant's third appearance, the credits have finished and Hawks allows the film proper to begin. The humour of the moment turns partly on the confusion between Grant and his character, the actor having apparently taken Barnaby so much to heart that his early entrance in front of the camera is the result of his already having appropriated Barnaby's absent-mindedness. But the moment is also a shared joke between Grant, Hawks and the audience, who are all fully aware that the real Cary Grant has made no such mistake but is playing at Grant becoming Barnaby too soon. The self-consciousness of this enactment – so clearly scripted and as much a part of the film as anything else – is part of a broader strategy by which the film's space is simultaneously the space of the film's narrative world and that of the film set on which it was made. Thus, Grant's entrance and Hawks's response show the actor at once attempting to step into the narrative world and presenting himself to Hawks's waiting camera. The kindly presence of the director just beyond the borders of the frame, protecting the enacted actor (Grant as Grant) from any gaffes or mis-steps, serves from the beginning as an assurance that all will be well.

Once the film proper begins, we see that the eagerness of Grant as Grant to present himself to the camera is countered by the reluctance of Grant as Barnaby to step outside the house to go dancing with his dolled-up wife, Edwina. He is too caught up in his own thoughts to do anything but take literally her instructions to turn on the porch light, turn off the hall light inside and lock the door, while she starts the car, but she has neglected to remind him to come outside before he locks the door. That they end up on different sides of it is a recurring motif in the film, one of whose aims is that, by the final shot, both of them should be inside the house together with the front door firmly closed, leaving us outside. Two of the melodramatic films considered in the course of Chapter Two – *Bigger than Life* and, more briefly, *The Searchers* – also begin with a door opening and end with one closing. However, whereas in *Bigger than Life* Ed Avery (unlike the children who rush out of the school in its opening moments) is trapped both at the beginning of the film (in the classroom) and at its end (in the hospital room with his family), Ethan Edwards in *The Searchers* finds himself – initially and ultimately – outside. If Ed and Ethan remain relatively untransformed in the course of their films in this respect, except to become even more emphatically confirmed and located in their original roles and spaces, Barnaby, by contrast, is no longer quite the same. For one thing, his absent-mindedness – the desire to transport himself imaginatively to another place – has disappeared.

Our original sense of a mismatch between Barnaby and Edwina derives not just from her desire to go out and his to stay at home – the closed door between them an apt indication of their separate agendas – but in Edwina's indulgent treatment of him as though he were a dependent child. When he misplaces his key, she tells him that he usually 'hides' it in his jacket pocket (as a naughty child might?); Barnaby's reply that he puts it there so that he can find it constitutes his first mild protest against this patronising view of him. As the realisation dawns that they were meant to go out, he takes her indulgence of his absent-mindedness – her failure to bring it to his attention – as evidence of a shared state of mind between them ('Holy smokes, we forgot all about the party'), though this is immediately cancelled by his sense that she does, after all, have a greater affinity with the present place and time, and he offers another mild rebuke of her for treating him like a forgetful child: 'Why didn't you remind me?' As they appear about to kiss, she asks him how he likes his eggs ('You're hungry, aren't you?', as indeed he is, though in a deeper sense), providing him with food instead of the nourishment he requires. As she serves up the meal, an apron replacing the party dress which she's now removed, it is small wonder that the following exchange ensues:

> *Barnaby:* Do you remember our honeymoon?
> *Edwina:* Of course I do, darling . . .
> *Barnaby: [almost to himself]* I was hoping you would.
> *Edwina:* . . . put those over there.

The last ingredient in this expository scene is Edwina's former suitor, Hank Entwhistle (Hugh Marlowe), who stops by to see why they've changed their minds about going out. Barnaby, who was so oblivious to what was going on around him in the earlier moments of the scene, now realises – as his wife does not – that her apron, which covers her adequately in front, has left the rest of her exposed. The piece of comic business whereby Barnaby tries to cover her up with a hopelessly inadequate dishcloth provides a clue to his own conflicting desires, wanting to protect her from Hank's gaze while enjoying the view for himself. He gets his wish when Hank leaves and he and Edwina 'stay home from the Everett-Winston party' (a reference to a long-ago party they failed to attend, and their euphemism for what they did instead).

I've concentrated on this opening scene in so much detail because the issues that will be raised later are all already in evidence: Hawks's benevolence as director, keeping his stars (and their characters) 'safe'; the ambivalence of the setting as simultaneously film set and narrative world; the mismatched married couple who need to be transformed (Edwina, on the one hand, by ceasing to treat Barnaby as a helpless child and by feeding his sexual hunger rather than his hunger for food, and Barnaby, on the other hand, by exchanging his absent-minded desire to be in another place for a desire to be on the same side of the door as Edwina, that is to say, in this place now); and, finally, Hank's status as an obstacle in the way of their reunion. That Barnaby and Edwina do manage to 'stay home from the Everett-Winston party' at the end of the scene, after what has clearly been a long hiatus, is a promising start.

The main joke of the film is that the formula invented by Barnaby is in fact useless, its apparent dramatic effects the result of a mixture put together by Esther, one of the laboratory chimpanzees, who, unknown to anyone else, has placed her concoction in the water cooler in the laboratory where Barnaby works. Until this is revealed to the various characters near the end of the film, we alone share this knowledge with Esther (and, of course, with Hawks offscreen), which suggests that the film's characters are the puppets not only of Hawks as director but of the chimpanzee as playful manipulator within the film, making monkeys of them all. However, although this may sound as if the transformation of Barnaby and Edwina which makes them appropriate objects of each other's desires is a regression from a 'civilised' human state to a more 'natural' animal one, what is actually happening is more a reversal than a regression, with the chimpanzee taking on a decidedly human role. Of the main characters, only Barnaby's boss Mr Oxly (Charles Coburn), with a surname that incorporates the name of an animal, consciously aspires to Esther's condition and behaves in a monkey-like way, his goal being to make himself an appropriate suitor for his secretary, Miss Laurel (Marilyn Monroe). This mismatch is unredeemable by the film, a project obviously doomed from the start. In Barnaby's and Edwina's case, their regression is expressed, above all, in terms of age, and the film's goal is by no means to lock them in a state of perpetual youth or childhood (for this, as we've seen in Edwina's treatment of her husband as a child, is part of the problem, not its solution), but to give them an alternative way of growing up and an alternative adulthood to grow up into.

Under the influence of the 'formula' (the term suggesting the milk available as a modern means of feeding babies, and also perhaps, reminding us of the Hawks film *Bringing Up Baby* in which Cary Grant's character has moments of regression to more animal-like states and behaviour), Edwina and Barnaby undergo a series of regressions to younger states. Although they first try the formula separately, Edwina entering her drug-induced state just as Barnaby has emerged from his (another version of their being on opposite sides of various doors, here metaphorically), a number of parallels between their respective experiments emerge: at the most superficial level, both Barnaby and Edwina adopt new hairstyles and clothes and take to the road, and each

Monkey Business. Edwina (Ginger Rogers) and Barnaby (Cary Grant): 'Barney, don't go to sleep. This is our *song*.' Barnaby locked out of the bedroom.

becomes dreamy-eyed when hearing 'their' song, though its special significance is lost on their companions (Miss Laurel in the case of Barnaby, and, more humorously, Barnaby himself when Edwina is under the influence of the drug and a drowsy Barnaby is trying to keep up with her on the dance floor of the Pickwick Arms Hotel: 'Barney, don't go to sleep. This is our *song*').

The formula releases not just a generalised version of their desires (as in Barnaby's explanation of his flushed appearance to his laboratory assistant, Jerome: 'Oh, well, that's probably due to my natural excitement'), but their desires specifically for each other (as when Barnaby, in the course of his regression, tells Edwina of his wish to stay home from another party with her, or when Edwina, in the course of *hers*, declares with romantic anticipation, 'Oh, Barney, it's gonna be our honeymoon night all over again!'). The symmetry – but non-simultaneity – of their desires to go back to a better time and start again is a sign of the potential for them to come together in the course of the film, but, for the moment, this possibility is blocked both by their unsynchronised explorations of the drug's effects and by the resentments which have built up between them and which, along with their desires, are let loose by the formula.

Edwina manufactures an argument over nothing, wilfully misreading Barnaby's words as they exchange the dance floor for the honeymoon suite. Or is it an argument over his sleeping through their song, another indication of his wanting to be somewhere other than on the dance floor with her? If so, it is reminiscent of the sequence immediately following on from the opening credits when, on the brink of going out dancing with her, he'd locked the door with himself inside, a connection confirmed by another repetition before they enter the hotel bedroom, when Edwina finds the key to the honeymoon suite in his pocket, after which she asks him if he's sure that he loves her – a logical continuation of this train of thought. The predictable conclusion of the argument she has provoked is that she refuses him her bed, locking Barnaby out of the room in his pyjamas and without his glasses. After his plaintive entreaty, 'Oh, let me in, Edwina, let me in'– an implicit version of which runs through most of the film, almost as his motto (just as Edwina's is a variation of 'Barney, don't go to sleep', perhaps more accurately paraphrased as 'Don't drift off') – he loses his way and falls down the hotel laundry chute, to be rescued by the cleaners in the morning. If Barnaby dreams of being in a sexualised private place with Edwina, her refusal to let him grow into anything but an oversized child is met by his absent-minded flights to another place when the realities of his marriage let him down, and this absent-mindedness (for example, his inability to hear their song because he's drifted off, in this case to sleep) in turn provokes her sexual withholding: it is an unending circle in which each – whether literally or metaphorically – closes doors on the other. However, unlike the considerably more vicious circle of mutual oppression and withholding which structures the marital relationship in *Bigger than Life* (as explored in Chapter Two), the relationship between Barnaby and Edwina is capable of transformation.

So the first set of paired regressions has uncovered various resentments which the couple feel towards one another. The second set of regressions – this time inadvertently shared, as they sit together in the laboratory and sip coffee made with water laced with Esther's chemical brew – will be the film's attempt to sort them out. The first indication we have that Barnaby and Edwina are more in tune with each other than last time – or at least that they have the capacity to be so – is when the larger dose of the formula begins to take effect, and Edwina pulls a chair out from under Barnaby as he's about to sit down. Rather than his falling down as we expect, he balances with one leg crossed over the other one, as though seated in mid-air, and looks at Edwina in gloating triumph. This sense of them being equal – at least in rivalry – continues as they splash each other with paint on the way home. Once they arrive home, the playing out of their separate resentments splits their fantasies in two, as Barnaby changes his paint-splashed clothes and joins a group of children dressed up as Indians in the grassy area behind the row of houses, while Edwina, after telephoning Hank to ask him to come round, falls asleep and is joined on the bed by a naked baby boy who has wandered in through the open door.

Earlier in the film, when Barnaby, under the waning influence of the drug, is becoming increasingly blind as he drives himself and Miss Laurel through the escalating dangers of the traffic, our exhilaration depends both on his obliviousness to the dangers that surround them and to our knowledge that Hawks (who, we remember, is watching his every move from a position offscreen) is not about to let him down.

Monkey Business. Edwina and the baby: 'Barnaby! Darling, speak to me!'

Monkey Business. Barnaby (Cary Grant), driving Miss Laurel (Marilyn Monroe), fails to watch the road, but a safe passage opens up.

Sure enough, just as Barnaby is about to crash into the vehicle in front of him, we see that the main bulk of its chassis is elevated above their heads, its wheels set far apart, and they drive under it – between its wheels – in safety. The oddity of this vehicle, whose only purpose is to guarantee Barnaby's well-being, provides a strange but apt symbol of the generosity of this film's world: in the case of the vehicle and of the narrative alike, a protective space opens up within it guaranteeing Barnaby's safe passage. Because it is clear that no physical harm will come to Barnaby and Edwina, our delight upon realising that their second dose of the formula will push their regression to new limits can keep pace with what now appears a perfectly logical development of the initial comic premise of the film.

The enthusiastic single-mindedness with which Barnaby enlists the children's help in his plan to 'scalp' Hank Entwhistle, and the readiness with which Edwina accepts that the baby beside her is her husband ('Barnaby! Darling, speak to me! Say something!') – an exaggeration of our earlier more provisional sense of their incompatibility when she merely treated him as a child, since she now actually takes him for one – provide the most inventive comic moments in the film, deriving from the eagerness with which they abandon the humdrum rules of decorum governing their everyday

Monkey Business.
Barnaby as 'Red
Eagle' prepares for the
'scalping' of Hank
(Hugh Marlowe).

lives. (I am reminded of the comic effect produced in Vincente Minnelli's film, *Meet Me in St Louis*, 1944, when older sister Rose/Lucille Bremer scolds Agnes/Joan Carroll and Tootie/Margaret O'Brien for a prank which has derailed the trolley car and could have resulted in someone's death. Given that it is clear that no-one will be killed, it is easy to smile at Agnes's dismissive reply, 'Oh, Rose, you're so stuck up.')

The simultaneous scenarios of Barnaby as 'Red Eagle', enthusiastically intent on revenge, and of Barnaby as a baby, completely helpless in Edwina's protective care, have the effect of presenting two opposed and alternative fantasies about him indulged in by husband and wife respectively. Barnaby's revenge on Hank (who, as the imagined object of Edwina's affections, stands in for the problem of her sexual disinterest in Barnaby himself) is a parody of a scalping: Hank's head is partially shaved in a Mohican-style haircut. Edwina's revenge on Barnaby for his apparent wish to be somewhere other than with her is a parody of their marriage, Edwina assuming a baby to be her husband in what is a logical extension of her having previously treated her husband as a child. By keeping him tied even more firmly to her apron strings than is the adult Barnaby in the film's opening scene, she thereby immobilises him in his wish to get away, though she comes to see the counter-productiveness of this strategy more clearly than before, as her dawning realisation takes shape in her comment to Mr Oxly: '. . . when he's twenty, think how old *I'll* be!' These comic actings out of their resentments seem to function not as temporary eruptions of unconscious material, but as exorcisms, and the memories of them linger, rather than being repressed. Thus, Barnaby tells Edwina, after he's recovered from the effects of the drug, that he does remember scalping Hank, while Edwina, rather than repudiating her fantasy when she sees the adult Barnaby lying next to the baby, is comically undaunted: 'Oh, Barnaby, darling . . . I thought I'd lost you, and now there are two of you!' Edwina's delight at the idea of the baby as her husband, while she nevertheless welcomes the adult version of Barnaby as a thing apart (splitting off her fantasy of him as a baby, in other words), and his satisfaction in remembering the 'scalping' of Hank, leave us with a sense of certain matters having been dealt with once and for all, and of the way having been cleared for a new version of their marriage where each is more fully present for the other, as they find in one another a home for their desires.

It should be noted, however, that much of the pleasure of these wonderfully comic moments lies in the whole-heartedness with which Cary Grant and Ginger Rogers throw themselves into their roles, treating as though they were perfectly plausible the most exaggerated excesses of the plot. It is clear that the safe comedic world where resentments can be dealt with through parody and through play is, above all, a world of performance. Thus, Barnaby reacts to his first experiment with the drug by doing a cartwheel and, in what is reminiscent of a vaudeville routine, walks towards Jerome arm outstretched as if to shake his hand, only to walk past him, arm still outstretched, as the telephone rings ('Pardon me, my phone's running over'). Edwina, too, becomes a performer, showing signs of the drug's effects by singing and clapping in time to the song. Later in the film, when she takes a larger dose in her coffee, its initial effect is to make her dance a few steps and pull the chair out from under Barnaby which, as we've already seen, produces a ready and perfectly timed response from him, resembling a well-honed comedy routine, a double-act between them. In the splashing of paint across each other's bodies, they come across like a pair of circus clowns, and even in Barnaby's incarnation as 'Red Eagle', the 'scalping' of Hank Entwhistle is preceded by a war dance and a song which Barnaby orchestrates skilfully amongst the children, their shared concentration and zealous involvement giving the scene a feeling of spontaneity and charm. The difficulty in disentangling the actors from the characters – in deciding whether we are witnessing Cary Grant's enthusiasms and delights or Barnaby Fulton's, say – is particularly marked when Barnaby lies down next to the baby and the baby makes an inquisitive sound whose unscripted spontaneity is evident, Barnaby's response ('Uh, no, no, please, no familiarity, just . . . just go to sleep') having the quality of an improvisation on the part of Cary Grant. It should be noted, too, that, in both instances of Barnaby's regression, he removes his glasses when his eyesight is restored by the drug, thus revealing his handsome looks and confirming his identity as Cary Grant behind the façade of Barnaby.

The degree of progressiveness in the film's ending is open to question. Thus, for example, Robin Wood has suggested that, 'The final resolution is simple and beautiful . . . There is no pretence that anything has been solved . . . but the two face their lives in a spirit of acceptance. Barnaby seems rather more purposeful and in control of things, Edwina less maternal . . .' (Robin Wood, *Howard Hawks*, revised edition, BFI, 1981, pp.82-83), whereas Andrew Britton insists, 'There is nothing here of the reconciliation of alienated sexual energy and "refinement" [. . .] *Monkey Business* is an extraordinary work, but by 1952 the exhilaration of release in screwball comedy has lost, irretrievably, its utopian dimension' (*Cary Grant: Comedy and Male Desire*, Tyneside Cinema, 1983). The drug brings out what Wood calls 'a sense of dangerous uncontrol' and what Britton calls 'retributive violence', and it is clear that the film is not advocating either state. When Barnaby takes the drug for the first time and offers a toast, 'To X58 and a better world', what he seeks is very different from what he finds – in his words, 'Maladjustment, near-idiocy and a series of low-comedy disasters . . .' – and at the end of the film he tells Edwina of his new formula, which will replace Esther's concoction: 'You're old only when you forget you're young . . . It's a word you keep in your heart, a light you have in your eyes, someone you hold in your arms.' But, before we dismiss too hastily the cloying triteness of his words, it is important to note the way Grant delivers them, his arms crossed, his tones ironic, suggesting that what he offers is just another kind of 'formula', and that he knows it – neither chemical mixture nor baby's milk, but cinematic cliché.

The safety of the narrative world – our sense that nothing bad will happen to the characters about whom we care (and, indeed, even a peripheral character like Hank loses only his hair, not his scalp) – goes some way towards transforming it into a better place than we have found in examples of melodramatic films. However, this aspect of the narrative world is a function of its status as a film, rather than as a social space, with Hawks as offscreen guarantor that this world is safe. But safe for what? At the end of the film, Barnaby remains the breadwinner, and nothing much has changed in the social fabric of this place, though he has relinquished any prospects of fame and glory to Esther, the playful chimpanzee who has now been put to work offscreen ('They've got Esther working awfully hard'). What was previously a matter of play for Esther has been turned to work, and Barnaby's work, by contrast, has become a bit more like play, as the new contract he'd hoped for at the beginning of the film has now been granted. Its terms are those he and Edwina had outlined to Hank in the first scene, when Barnaby described the anticipated improvement in his prospects as constituting 'a pretty good job':

> *Edwina:* Yeah, no more commercial assignments, no more working on non-skid girdles or noiseless popcorn bags.
> *Barnaby:* Yes, a roving commission, select my own field of research, exchange ideas with other professors all over the world, including a percentage.

But this alone is hardly a transformation of the narrative world as a social space, especially where Edwina is concerned. Rather, what we're given in the most delightful moments of the film is its transformation into a space where theatrical improvisation, on the part of the characters, and cinematic inventiveness, on that of Hawks, have free rein.

The most positive thing we are left with in terms of the film's social fabric is the sense of a homecoming between husband and wife, the renewal of a relationship of sexual reciprocity which feels safe but knows nothing of Hawks (who is hard at work offscreen, like Esther, manufacturing other people's dreams). Barnaby and Edwina have finally closed the door in the camera's face as they retreat from the larger world. This world, while safe, continues to be based on traditional social hierarchies, so their retreat into the home feels a bit like an escape, but one which lacks the claustrophobia of the final moments of *Bigger than Life*. In line with the requirements of the plot, Barnaby keeps his glasses on during his final embrace with Edwina, no longer presenting himself to the camera as Cary Grant, but fully immersed in the narrative world whose terms are the only ones Barnaby and Edwina can know. In this context, their rejuvenated sexual relationship, in which they meet as equals within the private domestic space, is the only attainable version of the safety of the larger comedic world guaranteed by the benevolent presence of Hawks outside.

COMEDIES OF MALE HEROICS

In offering *Monkey Business* as an example of a comedy of regression, I suggested that its comedic aspect depended upon the central male character, Barnaby Fulton, being seen to benefit from his falling away from a traditional version of manhood. It is not so much that the regression to childhood is presented as an end in itself, but rather that it allows him to grow into manhood in an alternative way, at least up to a point, so that in place of his absent-minded fantasies of being away from his wife in the world of work and professional success, he can come home to her both literally and metaphorically, unthreatened and unfrustrated in his desires, which are matched by her own. Of course, there are numerous ways of being something other than a mainstream adult male: one can regress from adulthood to childhood, as we've seen, but also, more generally, from a position of status and dignity to one of marginality (e.g. *Trading Places*, John Landis, 1983), from wealth to poverty (e.g. the Preston Sturges film, *Sullivan's Travels*, 1941), or even from being male to being female (e.g. Blake Edwards's comedy, *Switch*, 1991). Women, too, can regress, if not in terms of their sex, then certainly in terms of class or status (e.g. Garry Marshall's *Overboard*, 1987). The one essential which all of these examples share is that the regression involves a loss or abandonment of socially sanctioned markers of power, of whatever kind, and that the retrieval of something like one's former position involves a breaking down of earlier hierarchies of power, at least at the personal level, in the light of what has been learned, a breaking down which is seen positively and which the character undergoing the process of regression and retrieval comes to enjoy. Comedies of regression, as I understand them, are films about a second chance, a chance to be better than one was before, and in ways which feel better for those who are thus improved: the moral growth in question is not a punitive or self-denying transformation, but typically brings as its reward relationships based on greater generosity and mutuality of desire.

In Chapter Four, we'll be looking at films centred on romantic fresh starts, but we shall find that, unlike comedic regressions, the melodramatic versions of this theme do not so much involve regression (a going back in order to go forward) as a more straightforward progression where a previous identity is wiped out in order that its consequences can be escaped, and the new persona can adapt to the demands of a melodramatic world (a change which sometimes takes the form of playing dead and being 'reborn' in another part of the same melodramatic world). At the risk of oversimplification, it could be said that the opportunities provided by the world of comedies of regression contrast with the demands of the world of melodramatic fresh starts. While a malign fate seems to preside over the narrative world of romantic melodrama, a more magical and benevolent spirit seems to guarantee the safety of the central protagonists of comedic regression, in large part by establishing that what would otherwise be a melodramatic world is transformable in ways in which the world outside the film is not. Thus, comedic films that use regression as a strategy both uphold the illusion that their worlds are continuous with our own (the minimally realist assumption on which all mainstream American films depend) and yet make it clear that they are fictions, thereby revealing themselves, at the same time, as films. In melodramatic films that centre upon romantic fresh starts, the malign fate which governs their narrative worlds seems to inhabit those worlds (whether as social strait-jacket, as psychological determinism, as narrative dead-end . . .). In contrast, the spirit of benevolence which governs comedic films does not seem to inhabit them, but, rather, to be poised just outside, their characters unaware of its dominion.

It might be said that, just as Hawks waits patiently offscreen as Barnaby's benevolent protector in *Monkey Business*, so the offscreen directors of melodramatic films could, by contrast, be taken to personify the less benevolent fate which awaits the characters of such films. In offering us characters with whom to identify or about whom to care, however, both melodramatic and comedic films necessarily solicit our sympathy for them, at least to an extent – if we don't care for the characters at all, much less identify more closely with them, then the events which befall them are less likely to hold our attention for very long – so that films which offer them to us as suitable objects of sympathy, whatever their flaws, appear to be at least partially on their side. I am not claiming that melodramatic villains are always sympathetic (though many of them are), but insisting, rather, on the sympathetic aspects of at least some central characters upon whom the repressiveness of the melodramatic world is seen to press with particular weight. Therefore, whereas directors of comedic films can represent comedy's spirit of benevolence and work their magic (without contradiction) to the benefit of figures of identification or sympathy, the melodramatic director, if taken as controlling the malign fate which awaits the characters on whom we focus our sympathetic interest, would seem to be guilty of a sort of betrayal or perverse manipulation, setting the characters up in order to bring them down. I am not denying that such directors exist. Rather, I am suggesting that the path of least resistance for viewers who want to avoid confronting the contradiction in a film's point of view (which may appear to wish the characters both good and ill) is to locate such oppressive qualities within the films' narrative worlds themselves while, at the same time, attributing the solicitation of our sympathies for the characters to a structuring presence outside. Furthermore, to the extent that these films provide a critique of the repressive world they represent and the structures which maintain its distribution of power, it is more appropriate to locate its social and psychological determinants within the fabric of the narrative world, and not to see them as aspects of the director (as, say, a malign presiding spirit offscreen). If melodrama shows us a version of the world in some sense as it is, rather than as it might be, one can hardly hold its portrayers responsible for its underlying conditions.

These issues are complicated and far-reaching, and it cannot be assumed that those aspects peculiar to comedies of regression will necessarily also prevail in the comedic treatment of male heroism. In fact, at first glance, fantasies of comedic regression and those of comedic heroism seem to be clearly at odds. If comedic regression involves a liberating renunciation of power in a world where such a transformation is rendered safe, then comedic heroism – or, indeed, any heroism – would seem to require an unsafe world within which to be heroic, and to gather one's own forces or powers in order to face off its dangers and its villains. Surely where there are no such threats and no such intention of standing firm, there can be no heroism either.

Ernst Lubitsch's famous comedy, *To Be or Not To Be*, meets such difficulties head-on: its setting – Warsaw just before and after its invasion and occupation by Nazi Germany in 1939 – could not be more befitting to villainy nor could what is required of the troupe of actors who are its principal characters present more of a heroic prospect. If this makes the film sound like a melodrama where an oppressive narrative world closes in upon the characters with whose fate we feel a sympathetic involvement, the problems involved in turning it into a comedy can be seen to present a challenge on several fronts. Were the Nazis to have been reduced to ineffectual figures of fun (and, thus, made safe), the heroism of resisting them would have been significantly devalued, and the use of Nazism as the film's source of villainy in the narrative world would have taken on a disturbingly opportunistic feel (a sense that any blundering scoundrels would have done as well), trivialising the danger they posed historically in the world outside the film and, consequently, of the suffering endured by those actually on the receiving end of their intentions as well as of the risks taken by those in active opposition. On the other hand, if the film's heroism were to have been modelled too straightforwardly upon such traditional heroic male qualities as strength, courage, self-possession and so on, then the comedic possibilities of a world where conventional definitions of manhood are questioned and transformed would have been lost. Is it possible to make a comedic film about anti-Nazi heroism, or is the most one can hope to come up with a comic film (that is, with laughs at the Nazis' expense) in what is essentially bleak and unyielding melodramatic terrain?

The problem of portraying heroism and villainy comedically is tackled in a number of ways in Lubitsch's film, and indeed is dramatised as an equivalent problem for the troupe of actors rehearsing an anti-Nazi play entitled *Gestapo* within the film. For the actors and their producer, Dobosh (Charles Horton), the problem takes shape primarily as a question of whether to go for historical realism or for laughs. Thus, when we first see the actors rehearsing – but before we know that what we're watching is a play within the film, and not just the film itself – Bronski (Tom Dugan), the actor playing Hitler in Dobosh's play, responds to the 'Heil Hitlers' of the other characters with a spontaneous 'Heil myself', causing the rehearsal to come to an abrupt stop as Dobosh objects and Greenberg (Felix Bressart) intervenes.

> *Dobosh:* That's not in the script.
> *Bronski:* But Mr Dobosh, please!
> *Dobosh:* That's not in the script, Mr Bronski.
> *Bronski:* But it'll get a laugh.
> *Dobosh:* But I don't want a laugh here. How many times have I told you not to add any lines? I want . . .
> *Greenberg:* You want my opinion, Mr Dobosh?
> *Dobosh:* No, Mr Greenberg, I don't want your opinion.
> *Greenberg:* All right, then let me give you my reaction. A laugh is nothing to be sneezed at.

At this point, one of the other actors, Rawitch (Lionel Atwill), accuses Bronski and Greenberg of being two 'little' actors who merely wish to enlarge their parts (to which Greenberg replies: 'Mr Rawitch, what you are I wouldn't eat'). Later in the scene, when Maria Tura (Carole Lombard) makes her entrance into the room wearing an elegant evening gown, Dobosh is still at it: 'Folks, I want everybody to understand this. This is a serious play, a realistic drama . . . it is a document of Nazi Ger . . .

[*turning to Maria*] Is that what you're going to wear in the concentration camp?' Once again, Greenberg suggests it would get 'a terrific laugh', although Maria's husband, Joseph Tura (Jack Benny), is less sympathetic: 'Sweetheart, the dress stinks', at which point she accuses him of being afraid that she's stealing the scene.

> *Maria:* Whenever there's a chance to take the spotlight away from me –
> it's becoming ridiculous the way you grab attention. Whenever *I* start
> to tell a story, *you* finish it. If *I* go on a diet, *you* lose the weight. If *I*
> have a cold, *you* cough. And if we should ever have a baby, I'm not so
> sure I'd be the mother.
> *Joseph:* I'm satisfied to be the father.

Numerous issues spill out from this somewhat extended example: the disruptive power of humour (Bronski's humorous improvisation disturbing both the rehearsal of the play and our illusion that we're immersed in the film's narrative world as opposed to a play within it); the petty jealousies of the bickering troupe of actors who will end up as the film's collective heroes; the two camps into which they appear to split, with Bronski, Greenberg and Maria Tura on the side of humour and improvisation, while Dobosh, Rawitch and Joseph Tura advocate a greater degree of seriousness and of playing within the rules (whether it is a question of adherence to the script of the play or the upholding of marital fidelity). Of course, Dobosh's production and Rawitch's and Tura's reputations for hammy performances hardly embody the sober realism they profess, even without the improvisations of the others. The difference between the two camps, perhaps, is in the deliberateness with which Bronski and Maria, with Greenberg's approval, disrupt the verisimilitude – such as it is – of the play, as opposed to the unconfessed over-acting of Rawitch and Tura and the betrayal of Dobosh's seriousness of purpose by the unacknowledged mediocrity of his script.

If Greenberg functions as a sort of chorus, advocating at various points the merits of having a good laugh, it is significant both that he is a Jew and that, later in the film when Dobosh at last embraces the benefits of improvisation and devises a plan for their getaway, Greenberg's opinion is repeated one last time, but with a difference.

> *Dobosh:* If we can manage it that Greenberg suddenly pops up among
> all those Nazis . . .
> *Greenberg:* It'd get a terrific laugh.
> *Dobosh:* No, it won't.

By placing a Jewish character like Greenberg centre-stage in Dobosh's scheme (Greenberg relinquishing his earlier role as spear-bearer to Tura's Hamlet in order finally to play a starring role), the film emphasises both the very real danger he is in as a Jew surrounded by Nazis, and also, as a consequence, his genuine heroism in undertaking the part; at the same time, however, Greenberg's status as hero is hardly enhanced by his possession of traditional markers of power (his Jewishness offsetting his maleness in this respect). Further, Greenberg doesn't act alone, and the communal heroism of the whole troupe further dilutes any sense of individual glory or – by the inclusion of Maria as an essential member of the ensemble – any exclusively male dimension to their courage. Indeed, what is emphasised above all else is their resourcefulness as a group in outwitting the Germans – their shared improvisational skills as actors. If a safe passage opens up for Barnaby Fulton in the narrative world of *Monkey Business* by virtue of its nature as a film, then, equally, the escape route through Nazi-occupied Warsaw in *To Be or Not To Be* is the result of the transformative capacities of theatre.

The film does have one stereotypical hero in the form of the handsome young aviator, Stanislav Sobinski (Robert Stack), a lieutenant in the Polish squadron of the RAF who first appears as Maria Tura's secret admirer, Maria having arranged for him to join her backstage during Joseph's 'To be or not to be' soliloquy in *Hamlet* (Sobinski's indiscreet exits providing the basis for a recurring joke). However, far from being introduced to re-establish a more conventional image of solid male heroism, thus compensating for Greenberg's Jewishness or Maria's femaleness or the collective actions of the rest of the troupe, Sobinski's stereotypicality and lack of depth themselves become jokes. His limitations are expressed, above all, in a complete lack of susceptibility to irony, a failure of imagination on an impressive scale: Sobinski is comically condemned to take everything at face value. This extends from his dead-pan claim that he 'can drop three tons of dynamite in two minutes'– and his failure to read its unintended double meaning in the inflections of Maria's dreamy response ('Really?') – to his naive belief in everything that he's read about Maria in the press, and the reassurance he gives her of his intention to fulfil her dream of settling on a farm one day, insisting, as evidence of his good intentions, 'You won't have to use that plough anymore. I'll buy you a tractor.' Her husband, for all his vanity and self-absorption, can hardly be accused of having an imagination impoverished to such an extent.

Where Joseph Tura falls short of the requirements of robust masculine heroism – or, at least, its traditional image – is in being the husband of an unfaithful wife (in any case, a flirtatious one, who, whatever the outcomes of her flirtations and despite her evident love for her husband, is certainly beyond his control), with the risk of melodramatic diminishment that this poses. Tura is spared the humiliation that would be his lot in a melodramatic treatment of the same theme, however, partly by the contrast between Sobinski's naive earnestness and his own use of humour as a compensatory strategy. An example of this occurs when Tura finds Sobinski in his bed – innocently, as it turns out, as he's merely hiding out in the flat after parachuting into Poland from England having been charged with the task of preventing the Nazi sympathiser, Siletsky (Stanley Ridges), from handing over names of members of the Polish underground to Colonel Ehrhardt (Sig Ruman), Chief of the Gestapo Office of Occupation. Thinking he recognises Sobinski asleep in his bed, Tura begins the soliloquy from *Hamlet*, and his suspicions are confirmed as Sobinski automatically stands up. When Sobinski tells Tura to keep his voice down, 'Shh . . . not so loud, you might endanger all of us. After all, we're all in the same boat', Tura rises to the occasion with ready sarcasm, 'Oh, the same boat, eh? Well, then, let me ask you something, as one sailor to another, what ill wind blew you into my slippers?' answering what is no more than a cliché on Sobinski's part with a piece of inspired comic bravura. Sobinski is completely outclassed.

The second thing that prevents Tura from becoming an object of ridicule is his implied pact with Maria to disregard her relationship with Sobinski until the scheme to defeat Siletsky has been put into effect ('If I shouldn't come back, I forgive you what happened between you and Sobinski. If I come back, it's a different matter'). His heroism consists precisely in his provisional acceptance of the unimportance of the rules of fidelity in order to extend to her, in the face of a common enemy, his trust at another level.

> *Joseph:* It's unbelievable, unbelievable. I come home to find a man in the same boat with me, and my wife says to me 'What does it matter?'
> [*A complicated explanation is offered which he doesn't begin to comprehend.*]
> Look, look, look, look, I don't know much about the whole thing, but is this Siletsky a real danger to Poland?
> *Sobinski:* A catastrophe.
> *Maria:* He *must* be taken care of.
> *Joseph:* And he *will* be taken care of.
> *Maria:* Well, who's gonna do it?
> *Joseph: I'm* gonna do it . . . And after I've killed him, I hope you'll be kind enough to tell me what it was all about.

In the end, they all do it – all of the members of the acting troupe, that is, Sobinski merely serving his purpose among them as a literal-minded man of action who may kill Siletsky but lacks the imagination and improvisational ability to be of much use in what is required next: a piece of theatre.

Although Maria's relationship with Sobinski has to be set aside by Joseph as an irrelevance until Siletsky has been dispatched, it is, in fact, the very thing that indirectly causes Siletsky's downfall. Sobinski's suspicions were first aroused when Siletsky (posing as a Polish patriot) obtained the names and addresses of anti-Nazi sympathisers from the Polish RAF men in London by offering to take messages to their families and friends in Warsaw, but showed no sign of having heard of the famous Maria Tura to whom Sobinski wishes to send word. This, in turn, leads to Siletsky sending for Maria on his arrival in Warsaw and falling prey to her charms. When the actors contrive to take Siletsky to deliver his list of names and addresses to Joseph Tura, who is posing as Colonel Ehrhardt at a theatre disguised as Gestapo headquarters, Tura has to put up with Siletsky's insinuations about Maria, thwarted as he is by having to play the part of Ehrhardt, while taking advantage of this feigned disinterest as best he can to sing his own praises in compensation ('By the way, I believe her husband is that great, great Polish actor, Joseph Tura'). However, his growing suspicions of Maria eventually give the game away, and Siletsky escapes from the office into the theatre's empty auditorium, eventually to be gunned down on stage behind the curtain by Sobinski. As the curtain rises, the actors watch in silence as Siletsky falls down dead in a self-consciously melodramatic tableau. Tura (now disguised as Siletsky) arrives at the hotel where Maria has been forced to wait with Colonel Ehrhardt's man, Schultz (Henry Victor), who now takes Tura to his boss.

Ehrhardt agrees to book him a seat on a flight to Sweden, though he objects to Tura's wish (as Siletsky) to take Maria as well, Tura having suggested that he meet Maria and make up his mind about her for himself. The complications multiply when Maria duly arrives later to meet Ehrhardt, and he reveals that Siletsky's dead body has just been found in the theatre, where the Nazis were preparing a performance

To Be or Not to Be. The death of Siletsky
(Stanley Ridges).

for the Führer's imminent visit. Maria, unable to let her husband know of this development before he returns to see Ehrhardt, mobilises the other actors to go through
the motions of arresting Tura as an imposter and taking him into their custody,
unaware that by then Tura has managed to convince Ehrhardt that it is not he who
is the imposter but the dead Siletsky. The improvisations of the various actors are at
cross-purposes here, but in one last concerted scheme – Dobosh's plan to use
Greenberg to distract the Nazi guards outside Hitler's box at the theatre – the actors,

To Be or Not to Be. Greenberg (Felix Bressart)
centre-stage.

with Bronski as Hitler, arrest Greenberg and take him and 'Hitler' away in the real Hitler's waiting car to the real Hitler's plane, stopping for Maria *en route*. She is at that moment the unwilling recipient of Ehrhardt's amorous attentions, despite her urgent insistence that she has an appointment with someone else, but the sudden fortuitous appearance of 'Hitler' at her door convinces him to beat a hasty retreat.

As with the film's treatment of its heroes, which involves a variety of strategies being used to prevent us from identifying them with heroes of a more traditionally masculine type, its treatment of the three main villains – Siletsky, Ehrhardt and Hitler himself – does not conform to a single model. If Ehrhardt is closest to being a simple figure of ridicule and gets most of the laughs, Siletsky is there to make sure that we remain aware of the dangers posed by the melodramatic world and must be killed (in what I've already described as a deliberately arranged melodramatic tableau). The transformation of Siletsky into Tura, once Siletsky has been killed and Tura has taken on his identity, reduces the reality of Siletsky's villainy to a mere memory, and the actors' various 'productions' progressively reduce Ehrhardt, Siletsky, and even Hitler himself to imitations. The real Hitler, however (obviously played by an actor in Lubitsch's film, but meant to be taken as real in the terms of the fiction), is a reminder not just of the dangers to be found in melodramatic films, as is the fictional Siletsky, but of the repressive world offscreen; he remains a largely offscreen figure seen once at a distance and once from behind which makes it easier for him to represent both a figure in the real world and a character onscreen. So the film's treatment of villainy performs three functions: firstly, it holds the Nazis up to ridicule, primarily through Ehrhardt; secondly, it expresses, through Siletsky, the dangers posed by the Nazis while also defusing them by transforming the narrative world into a self-consciously theatrical space; and thirdly, by keeping Hitler as a (largely) offscreen presence at the edges of the simultaneously theatricalised and cinematic space of the fictional world, it reminds us that, in the real world outside the film, the Nazis cannot be so easily dispatched.

The film has a few more jokes up its sleeve once the actors are safely on the plane to Britain with Sobinski at the controls, including a laugh at the expense of the Nazi version of soldierly masculinity when the German pilots acquired along with Hitler's plane, who imagine they're accompanying him back to Germany (or, at any rate, lack the independence of thought to imagine anything other than that which they're

To Be or Not to Be. Maria's latest suitor leaves the theatre at the end of the film.

told), are ordered to jump out of the plane by Bronski-as-Hitler and do so with neither parachutes nor hesitation. But the last laugh is at the expense of all of the men in the film who have succumbed to Maria Tura's charms – not just Ehrhardt and Siletsky, but Tura and Sobinski as well – when, safe in Scotland, Tura is given the chance to play Hamlet again. As he starts his soliloquy with a wary glance at Sobinski in the audience, another good-looking man in uniform stands up and walks out, to the bemusement of both Tura and Sobinski. So, in the end, the film sides firmly with Maria, and her behaviour can be seen, in part, as her resisting the attempts of the various men to define and contain her (from Siletsky's misplaced confidence that she will be an easy convert to his cause and Ehrhardt's patronising greeting referring to her as 'little woman' through to Tura's jealousy and Sobinski's eager readiness to see her behind a plough). The fact that she is shown to get the better of all of them and that we are encouraged to relish her triumphs at their expense is evidence of the film's comedic resistance to repressive melodramatic hierarchies and roles. Maria's resistance is thus aligned with that of the film overall, and the openness and lack of guilt with which she acts upon her desires provoke our final smiles.

ROMANTIC COMEDIES

As I explained earlier, I intend to construe romantic comedy as a mixture of the broadly romantic and the broadly comedic, rather than as a specific genre or generic hybrid (like a musical Western, say). Although there are various genres which may appear to occupy the same territory, I want neither to exclude from consideration films within genres which fail to proclaim such general affiliation (the example to which I keep returning in this connection is *Rio Bravo*, about which I've argued at greater length in my article, 'John Wayne's Body', in Ian Cameron and Douglas Pye, eds, *The Movie Book of the Western*, Studio Vista, 1996), nor to assume that all films generally taken to be romantic comedies by others (screwball comedies, say) are necessarily romantic and comedic in my terms, though many of them may be, of course. I have said all this before and don't wish to labour the point.

The first two sections of this chapter deal with comedic films involving male re-gression and male heroics, which may or may not have a romantic component, and examine the possibilities and difficulties they present. I would now like to look more broadly at what is involved when a film is simultaneously comedic and romantic, though, clearly, in many cases, this combination may well make use of regressive or heroic strategies as well. However, I have chosen as my primary example a film which involves neither regression nor heroism, but does contain a sort of romance: Preston Sturges's *The Palm Beach Story*. Like *Monkey Business* and *To Be or Not To Be*, *The Palm Beach Story* has a married couple – and not a courting one – as its central characters. Thus it differs from those romantic films which end with the marriage of its main romantic pair and which may seem – in their melodramatic and comedic incarnations alike – to signal a positive and transformative resolution. What such films do not reveal, however, is what the romantic couple becomes once romance has been contained by marriage, for the simple reason that they end too soon, though in some cases, where it is evident that deeper melodramatic structures persist, the

The Palm Beach Story. Left to right across double page: Shots 1, 3, 4, 9, 10, 11, 16 of the titles sequence.

'happy ending' is less convincing than in others, despite a superficial sense of resolution. *The Palm Beach Story* turns its attention to precisely this issue.

The film begins with the wedding of Tom Jeffers (Joel McCrea) and his bride Geraldine (Claudette Colbert), though the credit sequence, consisting of rapidly intercut images showing the events leading up to the wedding, deliberately teases us with their initial impenetrability. The sequence unfolds as follows:

Shot 1: A maid gestures excitedly on the telephone, then sees someone offscreen (whose shadow falling across her is all we're permitted to see) and faints, a freeze-frame catching her in mid-fall, then unfreezing as she hits the floor.

Shot 2: Cut to a minister in church looking at his watch.

Shot 3: Cut to a waiting taxi as a character dressed as a bridegroom and played by Joel McCrea rushes out and points back at the building offscreen behind him, the image freezing and unfreezing as in the first shot; a doorman helps another man to get McCrea into the taxi and to climb in after him.

Shot 4: Another cut gives us a shot of Claudette Colbert tied up in a closet, dressed only in a slip and with a towel tied around her mouth, partially obscuring her features, so that it's possible to mistake her if she's not already a familiar face.

Shot 5: Cut to the same maid we saw earlier, now throwing her arms up in the air, as the camera pans right towards Colbert in a wedding dress picking up a bridal bouquet and running out over the maid's unconscious body on the floor, the image freezing and unfreezing as before.

Shots 6-7: Cut back to the minister, and then to the waiting congregation, a man running up and gesturing with arms spread to indicate, we presume, that he has no idea what's become of the bride and groom.

Shot 8: Another cut returns us to Colbert in the closet kicking at the door.

Shot 9: Cut to Colbert in wedding gown outside a building (clearly a different one from the building with awning and doorman where we first saw McCrea), running for a cab and jumping up and down in impatience as she waits, the image freezing and then unfreezing as she gets into a cab.

Shot 10: Cut back to the long-suffering maid with her hand to her forehead, fainting yet again as the camera pans to what we assume are Colbert's legs emerging through a hole in the closet.

Shot 11: Cut to McCrea putting on his wedding clothes in a taxi (but seated next to a different man from before, when he was already fully dressed), as the credits end with Sturges's name as director.

Shots 12-15: A series of cuts gives us the minister, McCrea, arriving in church, the minister again, and McCrea again as Colbert arrives and the couple smile at each other and kneel down together.

Shots 16-17: Cut to the maid sprawled in a faint on the floor, and then back to the wedding with, superimposed on the scene in an ornate doily-like frame, the words: 'And they lived happily ever after', followed by another title, 'Or did they?', and a consecutive list of years from 1937 to 1942 as the camera tracks back from the scene and the film proper begins.

The film's premise as well as its ending are outrageous pieces of comic invention. Gerry has been married for five years to Tom, an inventor with no shortage of ideas (reminiscent of Sturges himself), but enjoying little money or worldly success. The rent for the Park Avenue apartment she and Tom share is in arrears, and the elderly 'Wienie King' (Robert Dudley), in the course of being shown around by the building's manager (Franklin Pangborn), loses his way, or, rather, finds it, into the privacy of Gerry's bathroom and bedroom and then gives her enough cash to pay her bills and buy a glamorous new dress. The ease with which her charms inspire his beneficence convinces Gerry to try her luck on a grander scale: reckoning that their marriage has gone stale, she resolves to divorce Tom in order to attract a man of sufficient wealth to allow her to get Tom's inventions off the ground (literally, as it turns out, since his pet project is a sort of suspended airport constructed of metal netting to be built in the air space above cities). She takes the train to Palm Beach, Tom pursuing her by plane and arriving there first (the money once again provided by the 'Wienie King', as well as the suggestion that Tom meet her train carrying a bunch of roses). By the end of the film, Gerry has ensnared the exceedingly rich John D. Hackensacker III, otherwise known as Snoodles (Rudy Vallee), whose sister Maude (Mary Astor) has fallen for Tom, who, in turn, is posing as Gerry's brother. Sturges manages both to extricate Gerry and Tom from their profitable alliances and to restore them to each other, while simultaneously ensuring that the airport will go ahead as planned and providing Maude and her brother with the partners of their dreams in the form of Gerry's and Tom's identical twins.

> *Snoodles:* I don't suppose you have a sister?
> *Gerry:* Only a twin sister . . . Oh, didn't you know about that? That's how we were married in the beginning, both being twins.
> *Tom:* Of course, that's another plot entirely.

Suddenly, the credit sequence looks very different. Rather than the twins being pulled out of the hat at the end as a mere plot device – though, in a sense, that is just what they are – it is now evident that they were already present at the start in the doubled images of Gerry and Tom before their wedding: Colbert tied up and gagged in the closet is Gerry's twin, while she is Gerry when dashing off in a taxi in her wedding dress; McCrea, bewildered at the disappearance of his bride, dashes off in one taxi as Tom's twin, but, as Tom, is seen hurriedly pulling on his wedding clothes in another taxi. So it now appears that it was Tom's and Gerry's respective twins who were due to get married at the beginning of the film, but Tom and Gerry took their places.

If we pursue this train of thought a bit further, we can make sense of the maid's telephone conversation and subsequent faint when she sees the offscreen figure in Shot 1 by assuming she is telling Tom's twin that his bride-to-be is nowhere to be found, or something to that effect (the twin's reaction to the call made visible in Shot 3), when, unaware that he has an identical twin, she suddenly notices Tom in the room. Tom, presumably after having helped Gerry to tie up her twin and put her in the closet, hurries off to the church, dressing for the wedding on the way, while Gerry puts on the bridal dress they've removed from her twin and dashes out to find a cab to take her to join Tom at the altar. Assuming this version of events, and that the maid doesn't know that Tom has a twin, it seems probable that Tom and Gerry have only just met in the run-up to their twins' wedding (there is some confirmation of this in Gerry's words at the end of the film, which I've already quoted: 'That's how we were married in the beginning, both being twins'). So the decision to hijack the wedding must have been a spontaneous one, a bit of fun that seemed a good idea at the time (otherwise, why not have a properly planned wedding of their own and let their brother and sister get on with theirs?). The fact that their twins, in contrast, do not end up married to each other suggests a lack of sustained purpose on their part and an inability to adapt to new circumstances, to the unforeseen. Thus, a more symbolic reading opens up from the playful speculations which the film's opening and closing sequences seem intended to provoke: a reading according to which Tom's and Gerry's twins are their other selves, unspontaneous and overly cautious, for whom a passive acceptance of practical contingencies outweighs the improvised surrender to desire to which their better selves must find their way back in the course of the film. This parallel between the two couples is reinforced by Gerry's justification to Tom of her decision to leave him: 'I'm very tired of being broke, darling, and feeling so helpless about having my hands tied' – one cannot help being reminded of her sister tied up in the closet in the opening credit sequence.

In some ways, the relationship between John D. Hackensacker III and his sister Maude, the Princess Centimillia, reflects in exaggerated form what Tom's relationship with Gerry is in immediate danger of becoming, not least, a relationship like that between brother and sister. When Tom confronts Gerry with the fact that the 'Wienie King' has given her the money for the rent, she replies, 'Well, you don't have to get rigid about it', and Maude describes her brother as being 'stiffer than a plank'. Just as Maude hopes that, for once, her brother wasn't merely being noble in picking up Gerry on the train, so Gerry asks Tom, 'Don't you ever get tired of being noble?' The idea of blindness is also a source of parallels. Gerry accuses Tom of having become blind to her – a quality that, later on, is seen to go hand-in-hand with the pretence she foists upon him of being her brother (thus, Snoodles comments that the compliments he wishes to pay Gerry are 'things that a brother's naturally blind to'), and the recurring motif of Gerry breaking Snoodles's pince-nez is an indication that he too is, in some sense, blind, or at least unperceptive. A humorous proof of this is to be found in a comment he later makes to Gerry. During the train trip to Florida, the members of the Ale and Quail Club have shot up the saloon car in a shooting match, marched up and down the corridors in search of Gerry with a pack of baying hounds and generally left a trail of chaos and disruption in their wake. When Gerry and Snoodles are on his yacht for the final part of their journey,

Snoodles observes, with sublime obliviousness to the realities of the previous night, 'There are a lot of inconveniences to yachting that most people don't know anything about. Give me the peaceful train!' Such parallels between Tom and Snoodles bring into sharp relief Tom's need to loosen up, to relinquish his duty in favour of his desires, and to come to see things more clearly, in particular, to recognise that Gerry is the object of his deepest desires, and not just a convenient habit like Snoodles's habit of jotting down expenses in his little black book.

Gerry, for her part, is less satisfied with what their marriage has become – particularly in terms of money – and more eager to escape the passive acceptance of her circumstances which seems to characterise her twin (or other self); she embarks on what she envisages as a series of liaisons, or perhaps an advantageous marriage, where deeply felt reciprocal desire is an irrelevance, a not dissimilar approach to Maude's lack of discrimination where men are concerned (as her brother tells Gerry, 'She goes out with anything'), which is most frivolously displayed in her relationship with the aptly named Toto (Sig Arno), who trots after the princess like an eager and dutiful lap-dog. Where Maude is severe with Toto for 'always hanging around', Gerry seeks reassurance from Snoodles that, were they to marry, he would not do the same ('Would you be around much?' 'Not any more than you wanted me'). Clearly both women are in need of men whose physical presence would be a pleasure to them rather than an inconvenience.

The view that Tom is the man for Gerry is clearly expressed not just in the scene near the beginning of the film when, the night before she leaves him to go to Palm Beach for a divorce, he helps her to undo the zipper on her dress, kissing her neck and carrying her up to bed, despite her protests at the impracticality of it all. It is also shown in an unexpected, almost magical way, through a dissolve from Gerry in bed on the train to Tom in a plane in the sky above her on his way to meet her (not directly above, one presumes, yet the effect of the dissolve is to suggest a protective presence near at hand). The connection between them takes shape in the image of the plane's

The Palm Beach Story. Gerry (Claudette Colbert). Stars in her eyes.

brightly lit windows superimposed across her eyes, appearing at first as a single bright light and implying that dreamy thoughts of Tom, as she lies in bed, can literally put stars in her eyes. That such stars are worth more than diamonds is what Gerry must come to realise in the course of the film. In this connection, it is also significant that, when Tom meets Gerry's train only to discover that she has got off at an earlier stop, he asks the porter whether she got off the train alone, and the porter replies, 'Well, you might practically say she's alone. The gentleman that got off with her gave me ten cents from New York to Jacksonville . . . She's alone but she don't *know* it.'

In contrast, the physicality of Tom's presence – the sense we're given that his is an intensely physical presence for Gerry – is crucial, given the lack of range in both the mobility of his features and the expressiveness of his voice for much of the film. His smiles appear only at the weddings which open and close the film and, on two occasions, the morning after he and Gerry have made love. Thus, the source of his happiness is the mutuality of his and Gerry's desires; her presence alone is not enough, as his long face throughout the rest of the film makes clear. This emotional restraint in McCrea's performance, as well as the even tones with which he delivers his lines, is a risky strategy which could easily have made him a figure of fun like the also-rans of so many romantic comedies who stand by, well intentioned but passive, while the heroine and hero have fun at his expense (Leo McCarey's *The Awful Truth*, 1937, is a good example, where Irene Dunne and Cary Grant run circles around the decent and unimaginative suitor played by Ralph Bellamy). It is difficult to put one's finger on why McCrea's performance as Tom works so well without making us lose confidence in his ability to provide what Gerry requires.

Perhaps Colbert's much more vivacious performance is part of the answer, McCrea providing a steadying influence which complements her energies rather than stifling them. The fact that, unlike Ralph Bellamy's character in *The Awful Truth*, Tom is fully aware of what Gerry is up to, makes his seriousness not so much a matter of earnest stupidity as evidence of such virtues as patience and tolerance which allow him to give her a little space and time to rediscover herself and her desires. Gerry's stated motives in seeking a divorce are both that she wants to help Tom financially by making a good – that is, lucrative – match and that their marriage has become mere habit, with little passion. Doubt is cast on both these motives by her evident desire to have money for her own sake, as well as for Tom's, and by the readily surfacing desire between them, even if Tom has to learn to pay attention to what he feels. Gerry's relationships with other men are characterised, above all, by their providing her with clothes (the dress provided by the 'Wienie King', the pyjamas supplied by a member of the Ale and Quail Club on the train, the extravagant wardrobe financed at little discernible cost to himself by Snoodles). She and Tom, on the other hand, push each other to various degrees of undress (and can thus be said to discover each other again at the same time as they are more literally 'uncovered') even as Gerry denies the strength of their desires: Tom loses his pyjama bottoms as he rushes after her to the lift in their apartment building, where she's making an exit for a quick divorce, and on two occasions Gerry asks Tom to help her unzip her dress. The second time, counterpointed by Snoodles serenading her from beneath her balcony as she falls back in love with her husband, Sturges has her sit on Tom's knees, his hands placed on her hips to steady her, a gesture which seems to me to

The Palm Beach Story.
Tom (Joel McCrea)
steadies Gerry on
his lap.

have a powerful erotic charge. He then spreads his legs and she falls between them into his embrace, turning to kiss him, but still mindful of the financial windfall that their love will deny them: 'Oh, darling, darling, darling . . . I hope you realise this is costing us millions.'

Of course, the dresses that Tom helps Gerry to remove are those provided by the 'Wienie King' and Snoodles respectively, in each of which one could say that she looks like a million bucks, particularly the first, with its richly metallic sheen turning her into a kind of emblem of material wealth, and thus the embodiment of a particular version of the American Dream of which John D. Hackensacker III – whose name clearly echoes that of Rockefeller – is the pinnacle. The form taken by the 'American-ness' of the enormously wealthy emerges more fully in Snoodles's philosophising to Gerry at various points ('Staterooms are un-American', 'Tipping is un-American', and so on), and an American flag flies between them on his yacht as she discovers exactly who he is ('Well, then, you're one of the richest men in the world' she says, more to herself than to him). Maude's later comment to Gerry – 'We can look for new husbands together. I'm thinking of an American at the moment. It seems more patriotic'– is a further indication, though more playfully ironic than her brother's platitudes, of the need felt by the very rich to construe their wealthiness within democratic parameters, particularly at a time when the Depression was still a recent memory and the war was a pressing reality offscreen.

Continuing to exercise her teasing irony, this time at her brother's expense, Maude tells him that he should marry Gerry and that she'd marry Tom in an instant if she had the chance. Snoodles replies that she would only divorce him within the month, and Maude responds with cool good humour and self-possession, 'Nothing is permanent in this world except Roosevelt, dear'. Her comment may well make us wonder whether Roosevelt, as an ongoing and steadying influence upon American society (and a restraint upon big business to boot) in the unstable decade leading up to when the film was made, finds a kind of echo within the narrative in Tom's steadying influence on Gerry's energetic attempts to escape from the constraints of indebtedness to the luxury of an extravagant life. This idea finds some sort of vindication in the way Maude contrasts Roosevelt's permanence with the instability of the life of quick marriages and even quicker divorces to which Gerry too initially aspires, before her return to Tom at the end; both Tom and Roosevelt are figures upon whose watchful and essentially benevolent presence one can rely. So the version of Americanness presented as a patriotic, but essentially selfish, striving for wealth (or husbands) is countered both by Roosevelt's radical reinvention of American society and by the model of American know-how and inventiveness represented by Tom Jeffers, his name suggesting Thomas Jefferson as much as John D. Hackensacker's suggests that of John D. Rockefeller III. Bill Bryson, in *Made in America* (Secker & Warburg, 1994, p.107), notes that Jefferson was not just a founding father of the country as a whole, but also instrumental in the founding of the U.S. Patent Office in 1790:

> America had a long tradition of productive tinkering. Jefferson
> invented a plough, which secured him a *prix d'honneur* from a French
> agricultural academy (though in fact it didn't actually work very well),
> and filled Monticello, his classical Virginia mansion, with self-invented
> contrivances designed to thwart small everyday irritants. (p.106)

Clearly, Tom's view of himself as 'just a flop' (a view which follows from a perspective based on the value of wealth alone) is not that of Sturges, an inventor himself, nor yet of the film. Tom's resourcefulness and ingenuity – and, more generally, the spirit of improvisation which led Tom and Gerry to marry in the first place and which they rediscover at the end of the film, throwing caution, and Hackensacker's millions, to the wind – construct him as a quintessentially American dreamer, rather than a flop. The scene where Gerry, while on the train, gets stars in her eyes as she dreamily thinks about Tom, confirms the rightness of their marriage.

However, if Gerry's enormous energy and Tom's steadying presence spontaneously combine to reinvent their relationship as a sort of marital New Deal, it is still not altogether clear whether the strength of their feelings for each other will once again subside, as it did before, and the final titles of the film repeat the question with which it began: 'And they lived happily ever after . . . Or did they?' Through the music we can hear the sound of breaking glass, reminding us of the ornament Tom broke earlier when forced to witness Gerry's growing relationship with Snoodles and suggesting another lapse in Gerry's fidelity to Tom. This implied infidelity is similar, in some ways, to Maria Tura's newest flirtation at the end of *To Be or Not To Be*, though in other respects they have quite a different meaning. Despite Maria's evident love for her husband, there is no real sense of desire between them in the course of the film. Unlike *To Be or Not To Be*, but similarly to *Monkey Business*, *The Palm Beach Story* is what Stanley Cavell (in *Pursuits of Happiness: The Hollywood Comedy of Remarriage*, Harvard University Press, 1981) calls a comedy of remarriage, which is to say (among other things and if I understand him correctly), that it is centrally concerned with a reconstituted intimacy and mutuality (mutual acknowledgment, mutual forgiveness, mutual desire), and a one-sided infidelity as the film's last word would be totally at odds with this.

It is possible, of course, to take the hints of strife and infidelity as references to their twins' respective marriages to Snoodles and Maude, the expressions of worried bewilderment on the faces of both twins suggesting they have been thrust unwillingly into unions based on the absence of any sort of mutuality (or 'conversation', to use Cavell's preferred term for a kind of festive marital intimacy characteristic of comedies of remarriage), having been propelled into these marriages as unresistingly as they were presumably coerced out of the idea of marrying each other at the start of the film. Alternatively, the sound of breaking glass may simply suggest a livelier sort of conversation between Gerry and Tom where their differences are aired openly and where the strength of the bond between them is sufficient not only to bear such demonstrations of occasional disharmony, but to embrace them as an added thrill. There is an echo here, perhaps, of the way the marriage between Nora (Myrna Loy) and Nick Charles (William Powell) in W.S. Van Dyke's *The Thin Man* (1934) is invigorated by Nora's insistence that her husband – a private investigator who has retired to a life of luxury on the strength of Nora's money – take up another case, a clear source of excitement for her ('My soul, woman, I give you three murders and you're still not satisfied!'). In each case, the couple are kept on their toes, either through a lively sense of each other's autonomy, for Gerry and Tom, or through the thrills of murder and mayhem in the case of Nora and Nick – antidotes to the prospect of a marriage falling into a state of mutual neglect through the husband and wife failing to keep each other's attention. In both of these marriages, the woman is the instigator of the male's awakening from an unexciting life, whether of habit in *The Palm Beach Story* or of monied leisure in *The Thin Man*.

Traditional assumptions about a woman's role in marriage are resisted by the wives in all three of the films examined in this chapter, though Edwina's attempt, in *Monkey Business,* to mother Barnaby as the only alternative to being ignored and subservient within the home is less openly resistant than Maria Tura's flirtations in *To Be or Not To Be,* or Gerry's attempted divorce in *The Palm Beach Story.* Gerry's refusal of the role of good wife ('. . . I'm a rotten wife. I can't sew. I can't cook') contributes to her determination to help Tom in less conventional ways – most outrageously in her plan to marry someone else – and also makes it obvious that Snoodles, with his traditional views ('The homely virtues . . . that is a woman!'), is the opposite of what she needs. If the ideals of traditional feminine behaviour are resisted by both Gerry and Maude, traditional masculinity, while not voluntarily re-linquished by the film's various men, is held up to ridicule in the person of Snoodles, and especially in the shape of the Ale and Quail Club, whose ethos of drinking and shooting is so disruptive and anti-social as to lead to its members being confined to their private carriage, which is then forcibly abandoned in a railway siding, while the rest of the train continues to Florida without them.

As is also the case in *Monkey Business,* patriarchal figures of money and power are ridiculed and presented as figures of fun (Oxly in the Hawks film, the Ale and Quailers and Snoodles in the Sturges), while the central husband of each film (Barnaby, Tom) is sufficiently distanced from such status (through lack of career success and through a relationship of give-and-take with his wife revealing a potential for mutuality rather than bare assertions of power) to allow each couple a positive reconciliation once their privacy – which is another way of saying their intimacy –

The Palm Beach Story.
Gerry walks into the
'spotlight' on her
balcony.

has been retrieved. We've seen how Barnaby and Edwina need to end up on the same side of the door, while we, by the end of *Monkey Business*, are left outside. Similarly, in *The Palm Beach Story*, the intrusions into Gerry's and Tom's private spaces by others – the 'Wienie King' who invades their bath and bedroom, the Ale and Quail Club members who pile into Gerry's bedroom on the train, and Snoodles whose serenade provides an inadvertent accompaniment to the scene of Gerry's and Tom's reconciliation before they each shut the windows on him – need to be stemmed and their relationship reclaimed.

In both films, the reconciliation is a sexual one which does little to transform conditions in the larger narrative world, except in the sense already noted in the discussion of *Monkey Business* and *To Be or Not To Be*: that is, the safety of the narrative world is guaranteed through its transformation into a self-consciously cinematic or theatrical space by a benevolent spirit offscreen (Sturges, say). Thus, in *The Palm Beach Story*, Gerry's first entrance, once the film proper has begun, is onto the interior balcony of her duplex apartment looking down upon the manager of the building as he shows the 'Wienie King' and his wife around, the lighting contrived in such a way that Gerry seems to be walking into a spotlight. Much later in the film, as Gerry, Snoodles, Tom and Maude go dancing in Palm Beach, the chequerboard pattern on the dance floor reminds us that, despite their sense of free choice as they change partners according to their amorous intentions, they may still be pawns in somebody else's game. Snoodles may attempt to usurp Sturges's function when, at a suitable moment, he produces a full orchestra beneath Gerry's window to accompany what he takes to be their burgeoning romance, but he ends up performing to Sturges's ends as Gerry and Tom fall into each other's arms upstairs. He may have the wherewithal to pay for this extravagant production number, but Snoodles's performance as he delivers the song is unspontaneous – he reads the words, rather than singing from the heart – and he can't compete with Sturges's directorial panache in pulling the twins out of the hat at the end of the film.

Perhaps the only real rival to Sturges within the film is the 'Wienie King', who sets Gerry on the road to divorce with his gift of seven hundred dollars, and then sends Tom after her with a bunch of roses to bring her back. His philosophy seems closest to the values of spontaneity and risk-taking which run through the film, as well as tinging them with a hint of contemplative melancholy: 'Some day you'll wake up and find everything behind you. Gives you quite a turn. Makes you sorry for a few of the things you didn't do while you still could.' Indeed, Sturges uses him to point out the thing that even Sturges can't fix, when the 'Wienie King' replies to his wife's comment that the Jefferses' flat is as quiet as a tomb: 'I don't mind a little laugh. We'll be dead soon enough.' This intrusion of the realities of the offscreen world – the sense of mortality which invades an otherwise comedic world – is one thing Sturges can't keep fully at bay, though it provides the justification for the whole endeavour.

MEN AND COMEDY

I began with what I took to be a shared anticipation among film viewers that the experience of a comedic film will in some sense feel different from the experience of a melodramatic one. Where melodramatic films are repressive in the rigid hierarchies of race, class and gender which provide support for their version of the offscreen world, my hypothesis is that comedic films offer a series of transformations of this world and thus open it up to the expression of a range of desires which, in their melodramatic counterparts, are either repressed and displaced into violence or rendered threatening. Melodramatic hierarchies depend upon and are maintained by assertions of difference between characters representing various degrees of status and privilege, and are threatened by any fuzziness that may arise in the boundaries between the different sections of society implied in such a system, while comedic transformations either blur or reverse such socially significant differences, and are seen much more positively. In both cases, the romantic couple is the most common focus for such issues, since the mutuality of romantic love, while threatening the privileges of melodramatic men, at least in the private realm, holds out a promise of emancipation to those in the comedic world. Perhaps another way of saying this is that for those male characters who insist upon their privileges, romance poses the threat of a melodramatic world, but for those who are willing to relinquish them, it offers the promise of a comedic world. There is a two-way relationship, in other words, between a film's intended climate or tone and that which results *a posteriori* from the details of its realisation. Many films shift between the melodramatic and the comedic in the course of their narratives when intentions signalled at the outset come into conflict with their realisations.

A good example of a film which takes a particular interest in such shifts is *Sullivan's Travels*, which has the structure of a comedy of regression but, unlike *Monkey Business* where Barnaby is never in any real danger, plunges its film-director hero, John L. Sullivan (Joel McCrea), into a devastating world of poverty, imprisonment and loss of identity from which there seems little chance of escape until, through his resourcefulness in getting his picture in the paper so that he will be recognised and reclaimed by his Hollywood friends (and by Hollywood more generally), he is finally released and returned to safety (that is, to the world of film-making, rather than 'real life'). The lesson learnt by Sullivan as a result of travelling amongst the poor disguised as one of them (though, once he loses the markers of privilege which he thinks keep him safe, he is also assumed to be one of them with an iron-clad certainty he then can't dissolve) is that the only antidote to poverty and misery is comedy, which is to say a certain way of making movies. This film embraces a hypothesis not so very different from my own in delineating the opposing virtues of melodrama and comedy: though, by the end of the narrative, Sullivan has opted for comedy as his chosen mode of film-making, Sturges's film itself gives us a powerful glimpse of a melodramatic world of inequities, whose underlying conditions he is unable to change, in the midst of what is essentially a romantic comedy of regression, with only Sullivan transformed for the better, and not the world, except for that part of it which is the movies.

This has a very different effect from that of films which deploy the comic to provide the occasional laugh in what is fundamentally an unremittingly melodramatic world (for example, most of Hitchcock's films, as well as those instances of *film noir* where a wise-cracking detective, say, offers jokes in the face of a bleak and repressive narrative world) – a much more common strategy, I suspect, than the production of more genuinely comedic films. It is also very different from those films which, while failing to recognise the melodramatic nature of their worlds, offer us romantic resolutions as though they were happy while, in fact, they merely reinsert the couple into a gendered world of inequality to whose consequences film and characters alike are blind: that way lies sentimentality, and there are abundant cases in point. Some films – for example, a number of recent action movies – may even attempt to combine the cynicism of the first strategy with the sentimentality of the second, though the contradiction implicit in appearing to want to acknowledge, and yet, at the same time, refusing to know, the melodramatic world leads to instability and confusion. Thus, the romantic resolution of *True Lies* (James Cameron, 1994), for example, seems to require that its viewers suppress all knowledge of the nasty manipulations which have characterised the husband's earlier treatment of his wife. *Sullivan's Travels*, in contrast, has a deep and enduring awareness of the injustices of the world out there (both outside Sullivan's films-within-the-film, but within the bounds of the Sturges narrative, and beyond the borders of the Sturges film itself: that is, in both cases, beyond the means of the movies to transform them).

In looking at the three films which form the basis for the present chapter – *Monkey Business*, *To Be or Not To Be*, *The Palm Beach Story* – certain comedic transformations have become more apparent. Where the melodramatic world is a place of potential danger, the comedic world is, in some sense, safe (at least for those of its characters who share its outlook, though not for occasional villains like Siletsky in *To Be or Not To Be* or the thief in *Sullivan's Travels*, who knocks Sullivan out and steals his identity, along with his money; both these villains trail melodrama in their wake and die exemplary melodramatic deaths). In place of the threatening or frustrated desires of melodrama's repressive world, the comedic world is hospitable to the characters' desires and facilitates their proper satisfaction. Far from presenting us with rigid hierarchies of power based on socially determined markers like those of race, class and gender, the comedic is on the side of greater mutuality and improvisational play, its disruptive challenges sanctioned and seen positively rather than forbidden and suppressed. Finally, where melodrama's world seems ruled by a malign fate (usually generated from within, in the form of the structures and determinants of the narrative world itself), the comedic world seems to be watched over by a benevolent spirit off-screen (let's call it the director), who works cinematic magic whether through opening up a safe passage for the characters through the narrative world or through pulling such things as identical twins out of hats. More schematically:

MELODRAMATIC FILMS *are characterised by:*	COMEDIC FILMS *are characterised by:*
Danger	Safety
Repression, displacement	Expression, satisfaction
Hierarchical power	Mutuality, community
Rigidity	Improvisation, spontaneity
Malign fate	Benevolent magic

Neither category of films is intrinsically more valuable or more socially progressive than the other. The melodramatic potential for acute analysis of the injustices of the social world and the psychological mechanisms which distort and redirect its desires is no less rewarding an object of contemplation than comedic observations of human behaviour in the context of a more convivial world which, at their best, comedic films can whip up with strikingly inventive zeal. And, equally, a given comedy's implicit praise of cinematic magic is no less worthy than a given melodrama's implicit condemnation of the malign and socially determining fatality which is its presiding spirit.

At this point, we need to be more specific, I think, about the ways comedic films impose their transformations upon the various spaces of their respective narrative worlds. Because the male character's loss of melodramatic power within a comedic film is seen to be its own reward, he has no need of an 'elsewhere' to regain lost ground by violent means. Instead, comedic films work their magic over the narrative world to varying extents, whether only in the private context of the couple, or over the larger space encompassing the surrounding community, or over the narrative world as a whole. Thus, in *Monkey Business*, the entire narrative world is constituted as a place of safety in which, although its social hierarchies remain in place, they are all but meaningless. Barnaby's boss, Oxly – though he is ostensibly still in charge – is hardly a threat, but rather, a harmless figure of fun whose own silliness puts him in no position to demand a greater degree of decorum from anyone else; Barnaby's absent-mindedness and reckless driving are watched over by a benevolent Hawks who keeps him from harm; and the effect of Hank's 'scalping' at Barnaby's hands is reduced to the ignominy of a bad haircut. The narrative world is blatantly both a cinematic and a theatrical space, where the shape of a vehicle can suddenly appear to change (or at least our perception of it can shift and clarify) in order to allow Barnaby's car to pass safely through it, or through the space opened up within it, almost as if in a dream, and the effect of a potentially dangerous drug is, above all, a string of performances and improvisations with no long-term consequences except that it clears the way for something better later on.

When Barnaby and Edwina retreat behind closed doors in the final moments of *Monkey Business*, the private space they have carved out is very different from that at the end of *Bigger than Life*, when the door closes upon Ed, Lou and Richie: here the repression of Ed's desires, rather than their reawakening, is implied, and the surrounding world, far from sheltering them in its midst, appears to lie in wait with something like grim patience. *Monkey Business* is about Barnaby and Edwina together finding a safe place where being with each other matters more than either going to work (for him) or going dancing in the world outside (for her). But if the film is therefore, above all, a romance, and its fantasy that of the mutuality made possible in a private space within the social world, the safety of that larger world is what makes it a comedy; thus, the couple are protected by their placement within a social space that proffers custody and safe-keeping, unlike the rigorous ideological pressures and requirements that so corrupt the relationship at the end of *Bigger than Life* and sour its chances of providing genuine satisfaction for the couple.

In *To Be or Not to Be*, the safety of the comedic world does not extend as far as the narrative world as a whole: Siletsky, and, even more obviously, Hitler himself, pose very real dangers and expressions of power within the hierarchical Nazi organisation of occupied Poland. And in this case, the couple – Joseph and Maria Tura – are not the focus of the film's transformations; it is the community of actors which, by collectively creating a version of the threatening Nazi world where villains are replaced by their impersonators, and, in the process, theatricalising the melodramatic world of occupied Warsaw, manages eventually to secure the safe passage of the troupe out of Poland. The collectivity of the project (which, in the context of romantic couples I've referred to as their mutuality) democratises the troupe to the extent that even the role played by Greenberg – who, until then, had been reduced to a minor player – is as important as any other. So, a comedic film may transform its narrative world as a whole, providing a shelter within it for the romantic couple, where they may rediscover each other in a newly constituted intimacy, as in *Monkey Business*. Alternatively, it may provide a buffer against the melodramatic world which may be striving to intrude at the edges of the frame or narrative, a buffer in the form of a community united by common purpose and characterised by a greater degree of freedom from predetermined social roles and niceties, or at least a greater tolerance of such freedom in one another. In *To Be or Not to Be*, not even Maria's flirtations disrupt the sense of shared purpose, and the film applauds her lack of subservience to the film's men, just as it backs Greenberg's chance to move from the sidelines to centre-stage.

The Palm Beach Story shares elements with each of the other two films. Like *Monkey Business*, it is a romantic comedy in which a stale marriage is transformed into a newly wrought intimacy, privately and behind closed doors, unlike *To Be or Not to Be* which is punctuated by a series of dramatic entrances and exits, with Joseph and Maria never left alone and uninterrupted for long enough to renew their romance. But, like *To Be or Not to Be*, *The Palm Beach Story* goes further than *Monkey Business* in giving us a central female character (two, if we include Maude as well as Gerry), who is remarkably free of guilt as she follows her desires at the expense of those of the surrounding men (even if such desires need refocusing to reveal to her what she really wants: to be an adventurer with Tom, rather than an adventuress with anyone else, an outcome which feels nothing like a compromise or a defeat). Further, though the narrative world as a whole seems as safe and benevolent as that of *Monkey Business* – even more so in that the desires of all the main characters are met, and not just those of the central couple – Sturges still gives us some awareness of the darker currents of thought which motivate the 'Wienie King'. Although his meditations on mortality are not, perhaps, so very different from Mr Oxly's search for a chemical elixir of perpetual youth, in the case of the 'Wienie King' they lead to philosophical resignation and a certain generosity, rather than foolish and self-interested false hopes. Instead of presenting a self-contained utopian world, the comedic at its most sophisticated seems to acknowledge the threat of the melodramatic world, and its various strategies aim to defuse this or at least to keep it at bay.

It appears that there is no necessary link between whether a film is a comedy of regression or a comedy of male heroics, on the one hand, and whether it transforms the entire narrative world or only a limited community within it, on the other. Thus, while both *Monkey Business* and *Sullivan's Travels* use regressive strategies to strip away various signs of adult male privilege in their central male characters, the films differ greatly in the proportions of their respective narrative worlds over which their sheltering safety and benevolence extend.

Similarly, if we can class as heroic the willingness of Norval Jones (Eddie Bracken) to take the place of the errant husband of Trudy Kockenlocker (Betty Hutton) when she finds out she's pregnant in *The Miracle of Morgan's Creek*, then the film affords us an example of a comedy of male heroics where the narrative world and the benevolent community are virtually one and the same, in contrast to *To Be or Not to Be* which transforms only a portion of its dangerous melodramatic world through the heroics of its community of actors. The melodramatic potential of the plot of *The Miracle of Morgan's Creek* is clear: Trudy, while ostensibly out on a date with Norval, acquires a husband (under a false name while drunk), having met him at a party for a group of soldiers about to be shipped overseas; he disappears without trace in the early hours of their wedding night. However, a melodramatic outcome is ultimately staved off by the way the members of her family and community, after a series of comic disasters and misunderstandings which prevent Trudy's marriage to Norval from happening, gather round her protectively until the intervention of the Governor (Brian Donlevy) can set everything to rights. The character nearest to a villain in the film is the capitalist figure of the banker, whose vindictiveness is isolated and cancelled out by the generosity of the rest of the town. At the end of the film, the Governor annuls Trudy's first marriage, affirms the legitimacy of the botched ceremony marrying her to Norval, and (retroactively) grants a bewildered Norval the status of colonel in the state guard, the role of soldier having previously been denied to him because his nervousness had made him see spots before his eyes whenever he'd tried to enlist. In all this, the Governor's motive (a carefully considered one in the light of the publicity resulting from Trudy's having given birth to sextuplets) functions as yet another reminder of the cinematic nature of the film's transformation of the social space: while he is not an offscreen director, Governor McGinty is nevertheless a character from another Sturges film who is making a guest appearance here (he is listed simply as 'McGinty' in the credits) and he knows a good story when he hears it, merely embellishing it and the reputation of his state with the final comedic touches required to ensure a happy ending. Of course, he is also a reminder of the melodramatic corruption of big-city politics, though presented as benevolent (as long as his interests continue to be served) in the present film.

So there seems to be no obvious link between a film's specific comedic strategies and the extent of the transformation effected by the film upon the narrative world, but there does appear to be a connection between such strategies and the presence or absence of a convincingly eroticised romance. Where regression offers male characters alternative ways to be a man, thus making them suitable romantic partners for comedic women, comedies of male heroics tread a thin line between elevating their central male characters to a position of traditional male pre-eminence through their heroic acts and compensating for this either by displaying them as unlikely candidates for heroic standing in some other respect or by pairing them with women who are considerably more than a match for them, which makes for good comedy, but not necessarily for a fine romance.

That Norval is the ideal fall-guy – a solution to Trudy's problems rather than a romantic figure in his own right – is made clear both by his reaction when Trudy tells him of her short-lived marriage ('It happened that night? You mean the night you were out with *me*?' a mournful Norval asks in disbelief) and by the reaction of Trudy's sister Emmy when Trudy tells her how Norval used to go to cooking and sewing classes just to be near her, Trudy citing this past devotion to her as a reason not to exploit his kindness now ('But he's *perfect*', Emmy replies, 'He could do all the housework'). It seems that even the quiet heroism of a character like Norval, which comes down to a sort of basic decency in an otherwise unheroic and ordinary man, must be drained of erotic appeal in order to remove the melodramatic threat of a scenario in which a love-struck woman ends up with less standing and prestige than he. Though Trudy convinces herself that her gratitude towards Norval is the same thing as romantic love, the broad sweep of her desire earlier on for handsome men in uniform leaves room for some doubt.

One difference between Norval Jones in *The Miracle of Morgan's Creek* and James Stewart's characters, say, in some of his films for Frank Capra, is that the heroic decency of Stewart's characters is less tempered by comic ineptitude than is the heroism thrust upon Norval, and the relationships of Stewart's characters with women are, therefore, both more traditional and more melodramatic as a result. For example, in *It's a Wonderful Life*, the scene where George Bailey succumbs to his ambivalent love for Mary Hatch (Donna Reed) is characterised by an extraordinary blend of passionate desire and anguished desperation on George's part, and the marriage that immediately follows confirms that his destiny is to remain forever in the small town of Bedford Falls which he experiences as an oppressive dead-end.

My examples of comedic films have, so far, been drawn from the 'forties and 'fifties, but many of the same strategies and dynamics persist in more recent films. Before concluding the present chapter, I would like to take a brief look at *Groundhog Day* (1993), a comedy of regression of sorts directed by Harold Ramis. The film is centred on a cynical television weatherman, Phil Connors (Bill Murray), who, in the course of his fourth annual Groundhog Day broadcast from Punxsutawney, Pennsylvania, finds himself reliving the same day over and over again, though everyone around him, including his producer, Rita (Andie MacDowell), and their cameraman, Larry (Chris Elliott), is experiencing the day as if for the first and only time. Just as Barnaby Fulton, in *Monkey Business*, returns to childhood, in order to find his way towards a better manhood, so Phil keeps returning each morning to the day before, in order to remodel himself as a different sort of man, and it is only when he finally gets it right in comedic terms that time moves forward again. This process of self-transformation is inseparable from his integration into the small-town community of Punxsutawney which he at first treats with sarcastic contempt – '. . . they're hicks, Rita' – and also with unconscious irony, as in his comment that 'Someday somebody's gonna see me interviewing a groundhog and think I don't have a future', a prognostication which literally comes true, though not for the reasons he imagines.

As in other examples of the comedic world, the fate which befalls Phil, and the lesson he ultimately learns, seem to be the result of a benevolent spirit offscreen working for his benefit, and the cinematic qualities of his recurring day are echoed openly within the narrative itself. Thus, the film begins with a speeded-up image of clouds moving across the sky which, while unremarkable as a special effect in a film, has a magical feel to it as a narrative detail. This is followed by Phil presenting the weather forecast against a blue background, blank except for his shadow, in the Pittsburgh studio where he works, the television monitor transforming this background through televisual special effects, just as Phil's perception of the narrative world more broadly will be transformed by the ability of the film medium to rework the laws of space and time. When Phil is caught up in the second repetition of his day in Punxsutawney and he tells Rita he's reliving the same day, he replies to her question as to what he wants her to do about it by falling back on an image of his life as comparable to a television programme or a film: 'I don't know. You're a producer. Come up with something.' As he begins, still cynically, to use to his advantage his foreknowledge of what will happen, he sits, in the fifth repetition of his day, and, watches a series of events occur before him, intervening at the appropriate moment to steal a large sum of money being delivered to the bank, having described the unfolding events to himself like a film director plotting out a scene: 'A gust of wind. A dog barks. Cue the truck. Exit Herman. Walk on to the bank. Exit Felix and stand there with a not-so-bright look on your face. All right, Doris, come on . . .' and so on, the various characters responding as if in obedience to his directions. So the numerous repetitions of his day – of Groundhog Day, that is – can be seen as a series of re-takes in his own 'production' of that day. When he tries to exploit the knowledge of Rita's likes and dislikes which he's gleaned in the course of many repeated attempts to manipulate her into falling for him (as someone with whom she has much in common), he replies to her amazed observation that, 'It's a perfect day. You couldn't have planned a day like this,' with the truth, for once: 'Well, you can, it just takes an awful lot of work.' However, Phil still has a lot to learn before he and Rita can come together on more equal terms.

In befriending a couple of amiable drunks, Ralph (Rick Overton) and Gus (Rick Ducommun), whom he meets in the diner and later joins up with in the local bowling alley, Phil discovers as they talk that they have more in common than he'd thought:

> *Phil:* What would *you* do if you were stuck in one place and every day was exactly the same and nothing that you did mattered?
> *Ralph:* That about sums it up for *me*.

The sense of Punxsutawney as oppressive is reinforced and yet reversed in Phil's case, as it dawns on him that he can now do whatever he wants with no fear of the consequences, and that the enforced repetitiveness of small-town life in which he's trapped is, at the same time, a licence to transgress its rules. As he drives along with his two new friends, he contemplates the many rules he's now free to break.

> *Phil:* It's the same thing your whole life. Clean up your room. Stand up straight. Pick up your feet. Take it like a man. Be nice to your sister. Don't mix beer and wine, ever. Oh, yeah, don't drive on the railroad track.
> *Gus:* Phil, that's one I happen to agree with.

Phil no longer needs to live by society's rules nor to worry about his health, nor even to stay alive, and the exhilarating sequences of transgressions, self-indulgence, and even suicides – with Phil safe in the knowledge that all his actions will be cancelled in the morning, when February 2nd dawns again – are comparable to the various scenes in *Monkey Business* in which Barnaby can drive recklessly and threaten to scalp Hank Entwhistle with no lasting bad effects either for himself or for others. And, yet, in both *Monkey Business* and *Groundhog Day*, freedom from responsibility is also a freedom from commitment, and the romantic couple in each film is driven apart rather than united by such self-centred opportunism. As Phil tells Rita in the midst of his deepening despair, 'I'll give you a winter prediction. It's gonna be cold, it's gonna be grey. And it's gonna last you for the rest of your life.' A few repetitions later, his Groundhog Day broadcast is equally bleak: 'There is no way that this winter is ever going to end, as long as this groundhog keeps seeing his shadow. I don't see any other way out. He's got to be stopped. And I have to stop him.' Phil kidnaps the groundhog – his namesake, 'Punxsutawney Phil' – and drives off a cliff in a shared, but temporary, death, presented as a kind of self-conscious and excessive performance ('Well, we mustn't keep our public waiting, huh? It's show-time, Phil'), which leads in-to the sequence of suicides to which Phil now turns as his only way out. The reference to the groundhog's shadow, which heralds six more weeks of winter, is reminiscent of Phil's weather report in Pittsburgh at the start of the film, when only his shadow was visible against the plain blue background in the studio, in contrast to the tele-vised version which filled in the background through the 'magic' of special effects. But it is only in the diner scene following the montage of suicides that Phil's world is definitively transformed, as he fills in the scene's background in another sense.

This scene is the turning point in the film as Phil, in an effort to convince Rita of the reality of his predicament, introduces her to the various people in the diner, beginning with their waitress:

> *Phil:* This is Doris. Her brother-in-law, Carl, owns this diner. She's worked here since she was seventeen. More than anything else in her life she wants to see Paris before she dies . . . This is Debbie Kleiser and her fiancé, Fred . . . They're supposed to be getting married this afternoon, but Debbie is having second thoughts . . . This is Bill. He's been a waiter for three years, since he left Penn State and had to get work. He likes the town, he paints toy soldiers, and he's gay . . . This is Gus. He hates his life here. He wishes he'd stayed in the navy . . . This is Tom. He worked in the coal-mine until they closed it down . . .

Anonymous background characters are suddenly fleshed out, and Phil's knowledge of intimate details of their hopes and regrets is an indication, not merely that he's been around for some time, but that he's gained their confidence and listened carefully to what they had to say, even though this information could not be exploited in any obvious way for his personal benefit. If the diner – and, by extension, Punxsutawney – is transformed into a place where no one is marginalised, each character (no matter how subsidiary to the plot) having a story to tell, so too is Phil suddenly transformed in our eyes into a more sensitive and sympathetic character, his earlier position of cynical superiority replaced by involvement with others, despite the hints of mischief which still remain (in publicly announcing Bill's homosexuality, for example, or in revealing Debbie's doubts about marriage in front of her fiancé). This process of Phil's reformation continues throughout the latter part of the film, as he uses his privileged knowledge to help people, rather than to exploit them, and even takes up the piano, improving dramatically with each repetition of his day.

The culmination of this process is in the final version of the day, when Phil has become a sort of small-town hero, the comedy of regression with which we began having seamlessly turned into a comedy of male heroics. The first thing we see is Phil's broadcast once again, with Phil refuting Chekhov's vision – also, until recently, his own – of a bleak dark winter: 'But standing here among the people of Punxsutawney and basking in the warmth of their hearths and hearts, I couldn't imagine a better fate than a long and lustrous winter.' Accepting the applause his words provoke, he dashes off to perform a series of good deeds, catching a boy who falls from a tree ('You have *never* thanked me. I'll see you tomorrow . . . maybe'), changing a flat tyre ('It's nothing, ma'am'), saving a man from choking in a restaurant, and so on. At the Groundhog Day celebrations that night, Phil, taking a break from his expert jazz improvisations at the piano, is the focus of everyone's thanks and attention, and described by Rita as 'the most popular person in town'. This is both an echo and a partial reversal of the end of *It's a Wonderful Life* where the townsfolk of Bedford Falls crowd around George Bailey – whose brother calls him 'the richest man in town', in friends if not in money – and for once offer him their help, rather than asking for his.

At last, Phil and Rita can have their romance and he can admit his love for her with something like sincerity, and the day can finally draw to a close. Of course, this brings with it an end to his prescience as well, the resulting loss of future heroic possibilities yet again an apparent condition of comedic romance. To see the film as sentimental in its redemption of a self-interested cynic is to underrate the sly ironies of Bill Murray's performance and the many humorous details both in the film's narrative events and in its script, not least in Phil's final throwaway line as he and Rita kiss: 'It's so beautiful. Let's live here . . . We'll rent to start.' As with Barnaby Fulton's ironic recipe for being young at heart at the end of *Monkey Business*, which he recites with some knowingness as a formula and nothing more, so Phil is aware that the idealised version of small-town life in Punxsutawney may be just another cliché, his commitment to it hedged by keeping open an escape route just in case.

CHAPTER FOUR

ROMANTIC FRESH STARTS

An Affair to Remember

I observed earlier that romance is rarely free-standing and that to classify a film in this way – simply as a romance – provides only part of the picture. Romantic melodrama or romantic comedy? That is the crucial question. Is desire the ingredient that locks the romantic couple into a tight and repressive world, or can it in some way liberate them? In all of the films discussed in this chapter, the central male character is transformed in a fairly fundamental sense: in the words of Nicky Ferrante (Cary Grant) at a key stage in his reconstruction of himself in *An Affair to Remember* (Leo McCarey, 1957), 'The old Ferrante is dead.' The nature of this transformation and the role played by romance require careful examination. As we shall see in *An Affair to Remember*, it is not always easy to determine whether romantic films are essentially melodramatic or comedic, since to some extent many of them have aspects of both.

On the basis of the bleak shot of leafless trees in the falling snow with which the film opens, one can hardly be blamed for assuming that this is the story of a romance that will end badly. Indeed, the film's title itself implies a perspective of loss, the love affair reduced to a memory of events now faded with time. Reinforcing the impression of a frozen world retrievable only through the imagination are the words of the title song which accompany the wintry cityscape of trees and buildings, with the Empire State Building in the background of the shot barely visible through the snow:

> Our love affair is a wondrous thing
> That we'll rejoice in remembering.
> Our love was born with our first embrace,
> And a page was torn out of time and space.
> Our love affair, may it always be
> A flame to burn through eternity.
> So take my hand with a fervent prayer
> That we may live and we may share
> A love affair to remember.

And yet the words are decidedly odd. They simultaneously imply the early stages of a new romance ('So take my hand . . .') and anticipate looking back on it (a 'love affair . . . that we'll rejoice in remembering'), an invitation from one lover to the other to embark on the love affair not so much for its own sake as for the prospect of being able to look back on it later when it's over. This affair is valued not as an existing, ongoing experience but as a thing apart ('a page . . . torn out of time and space'), and the possibilities of remembering it depend on it coming to an end, and, even more importantly, on it not getting bogged down in the petty domestic messiness of everyday life. In these respects, the film is reminiscent of Max Ophuls's *Letter from an Unknown Woman* (1948), a similarity which is emphasised by Andrew Britton in his discussion of Terry McKay (Deborah Kerr), the female lead in *An Affair to Remember*. He points out that she can be compared to Ophuls's Lisa (Joan Fontaine) in terms of the adamant refusals of both women to contact their respective lovers to ask for help – Lisa after she has fallen pregnant and Terry after she has had her accident (*Cary Grant: Comedy and Male Desire*, Tyneside Cinema, 1983). Nicky and Terry are a bit like those tourists who are so engrossed in taking idealised photographs for future consumption in the cosy comfort of their easy chairs at home that they miss the many small details of life going on around them, and there is a parallel in the scene in Ophuls's film when Lisa and her lover, Stefan (Louis Jourdan), sit together in a fairground railway carriage and watch the painted backdrops roll by, although, at this point, Stefan is more detached from Lisa's romantic illusions than Nicky ever is from Terry's. Vic Damone's male voice on the soundtrack of McCarey's film suggests that it is Nicky whose point of view is expressed, but the song will later be sung twice by Terry, suggesting that their love affair is based on their shared perspective on romantic love and the need they both feel for a world of absolutes. Both Nicky and Terry are tourists in the realms of the everyday, the real world having disappointed each of them in different ways and needing to be imaginatively reconstructed through their shared romantic idealism.

The question arises, of course, as to whether McCarey's film itself is drawn into such an idealised view of romance, but we are immediately disabused of any such notion by a dissolve to Robert Q. Lewis (playing himself) as he announces to the television cameras the news of Nicky Ferrante's engagement to the enormously wealthy Lois Clark (Neva Patterson), after an item of purely financial news: 'And so, while the New York Stock Exchange showed signs of restlessness, there was little or no uneasiness on the part of optimists . . .' The emphasis on Lois Clark's 'six hundred million bucks' and the placing of the relationship within a straightforwardly ecomonic context expressed in quintessential American slang ('Not only all that lettuce but a beautiful tomato too') counteract the sentimental idealism of the title song and simultaneously signal to the viewer Lois's unsuitability as a romantic heroine because of this very contrast.

This underlining of the culturally specific dimension of heterosexual relationships continues with the Italian and British versions of the broadcast that follow, the Italian newscaster speculating on how Lois's wealth would translate into Italian *lire* and the British broadcaster reading the financial details to himself and discreetly omitting them from his report ('Well . . . [*he reads to himself*] . . . well, there you have it'). The Britishness of both lead actors – despite the fact that Cary Grant was by then an American citizen and plays a character of uncertain nationality with a French grandmother and an Italian name, and Deborah Kerr plays an American – means that, to a degree, they bring the same connotations of discretion and reserve to their roles, especially where matters of money are concerned. The sequence in its entirety represents a shift in tone from the melodramatic nature of the opening of the film to the comic, as well as a shift from universal platitudes about romance (in the title song) to stereotyped, culturally specific attitudes to love and money (in the various broadcasts). The scene dissolves to a shot of the ship bringing Nicky Ferrante

An Affair to Remember. Nicky (Cary Grant) and Terry (Deborah Kerr). Nicky, eyes narrowed, fidgets with his cigarette case.

and Terry McKay back to the United States and to their respective partners – Lois and Ken (Richard Denning) – who await them.

From the opening shot of the Empire State Building with its top in the clouds to the television broadcasts which bring us abruptly down to earth, we now find ourselves at sea, and this series of spatial metaphors continues through the film, reflecting very different perspectives on romance. That we first meet Nicky and Terry on board ship is suggestive in a number of ways. Certainly, it picks up on the image (mentioned earlier) of the two as 'tourists' unanchored in the day-to-day details of ordinary life. Although this lack of commitment to the everyday (and to the mundane relationships in which they're both involved) makes them ripe for a shipboard romance, which will blossom during their visit to Nicky's grandmother (Cathleen Nesbitt) in Villefranche, their acquaintance begins with a great deal of uncertainty. Their early conversations, while reminiscent of the playful interchanges of romantic comedy, are brittle, the playfulness calculated and defensive. In this context, Cary Grant's careful articulation of Nicky's words when he asks Terry, 'What is your name?', giving equal emphasis to each syllable, conveys stiffness and formality, rather than careless charm, and the casual flattery of his comment that 'You saved my life. I was bored to death . . .' is betrayed by the way he fidgets with his cigarette case as the conversation goes on. Terry is quick to pick up on, and rebuke him for, the insincerity of his words.

> *Terry:* Tell me, have you been getting *results* with a line like that?
> Or would I be surprised?
> *Nicky:* If *you* were surprised, *I'd* be surprised.
> *Terry:* That sounds like a nasty crack . . .

His bitterness and her defensiveness are very close to the surface here and erupt rather too readily to be ignored. Terry goes on to offer joking rebukes about his womanising, and Nicky responds by asking why her male companion isn't with her. Her reply, that he's in Texas arranging a merger ('The big secret seems to be to merge a *sick* corporation with a big fat healthy one, and then everybody gets well'), foreshadows the film's resolution when she will be confined to a wheelchair and union with Nicky will finally take place, but, once again, the implication that relationships are mediated by economic factors contrasts with Terry's and Nicky's need to see romance in a more idealised fashion.

And yet the terms not just of Nicky's engagement to Lois but of Terry's relationship to Ken are clearly – and uncomfortably – informed by money, with both Nicky and Terry beneficiaries of their respective partners' financial largesse. Indeed, Terry's reluctance to tell anyone about her relationship with Nicky – even when it has developed into a firm mutual commitment – may represent a wish not to burn her bridges before he's proved his ability to support her in style since, as she tells him, 'it's the kind of life we've both been used to'. Still, Terry's disappointment in her relationship with Ken is evident from the start, when she shows Nicky the photograph of Ken in her cabin and he asks if he's her husband, Terry having to admit that he's not (her lowered eyes revealing her momentary uneasiness), though they've been together for five faithful years. When Ken learns about Terry's shipboard romance later in the film and tells her he wants to marry her and that he knows he should have asked her long ago, it is too little too late. Terry's response to Nicky's questions makes it clear that Ken's failure to propose and her resultant position as a kept woman are points of keen sensitivity and embarrassment, which she does her best to disguise with bright repartee. Thus, when she describes the job she had as a singer in a nightclub when she first met Ken and his reaction to it – 'Why, you don't *belong* in a place like this' – her tone is ironic and contains more than a touch of self-mockery, provoking Nicky's sarcastic reply ('Really?') as he takes his lead from her, in effect the last thing she wants, which sends her into confusion.

> *Terry:* Mmm hmm. And I said . . . uh . . . I don't . . . [*she laughs self-consciously here*] . . . And . . . uh . . . well, then . . . hmm . . . what?
> *Nicky:* What, what?
> *Terry:* I don't know. I thought you said something. Oh, I'm sorry. But you're right, you know . . .

She goes on to tell him of the Park Avenue apartment in which Ken set her up, but instead of receiving the reassurance about her worth which she seems to need from Nicky at this point, she is treated to continuing sarcasm – 'An ideal place for you to improve yourself' – eliciting from her a qualified 'Yes', her intonation indicating her reservations and reluctance to acquiesce in this view of herself. She talks of having studied hard to acquaint herself with the finer points of music, art, literature, and so on (a description echoed by Nicky's grandmother in Villefranche when she tells Terry that Nicky 'charmed us all with his piano playing, then he studied painting . . .'), but, rather than recognising himself in Terry's remark, his reply is, again, an implicitly critical one:

> *Terry:* . . . I studied hard . . .
> *Nicky:* So that one day you'd make a perfectly charming wife.
> *Terry:* [*defensively, and with some assertiveness*] Yes, that was the general idea. Anything *wrong* with that?

His desire to keep seeing her for the rest of the trip, but for his own less-than-romantic reasons ('. . . I can't stand monotony'), and her wish that they go their separate ways, are indicative of his need to keep her at arm's length (treating her as just another of his endless stream of women), and of her growing acknowledgment of the loss of self-respect brought about by the relationship with Ken and her determination that it should be restored.

Nicky's defensiveness is less to do with the fact that he will be financially dependent on his future wife Lois than with his awkwardness when his usual line in charm and seduction fails to win Terry over ('Don't tell me you're embarrassed,' she says in ironic surprise, 'Oh, I am sorry . . . Oh I do hope it won't affect your ego . . .'). And yet, although his previous sexual conquests came easily to him, he seems to long for a woman he can idealise who will not disappoint him like all the others. When Terry asks him whether, when he was little, his nurse read him the memoirs of Casanova, her sarcastic tones are a match for the sarcastic remarks he directs against her, and Nicky narrows his eyes resentfully as he replies: 'Every night. And then we'd turn out the light.'

> *Terry: We?*
> *Nicky:* I was only so big [*gesturing*].
> *Terry:* You must have had a happy childhood.
> *Nicky:* Ah, yes.

He goes on to explain how he tends to idealise women who then let him down, all the time playing with his cigarette case as before, his manner guarded, in spite of his smiles. Whereas Terry seems to long for a total romantic commitment from a man to restore her self-respect, Nicky seems much more wary, as though no woman can ever live up to what he requires. The reason for this becomes apparent soon afterwards when, after Nicky and Terry continually bump into each other on board ship despite their best efforts to keep apart, he invites her to accompany him on a visit to his grandmother during their stop in Villefranche.

Nicky's grandmother and her perfectly enclosed world set high above the town represent everything Nicky and Terry have been seeking. As they ride uphill in a carriage, Nicky points out the view down below:

> *Nicky:* Isn't it beautiful down there?
> *Terry:* Yes, but . . . uh . . . do you want to hear an old joke? If it's so
> beautiful down there . . .
> *Nicky:* [*finishing her sentence*] . . . what did you bring me up here for?

Clearly we are back in the clouds again, looking down from afar at a vista of life and change rather than being in its midst. At last there is a setting appropriate to the requirements of romantic love, a world of frozen perfection, of detachment from the everyday world, and of absolute fidelity: the grandmother's dog is even named Fidèle. In Nicky's words, his grandmother, with her husband's grave so near at hand, 'must be waiting, I think a little impatiently, for the day she will join him'. Once again, Grant's inflection is stiff and formal here, befitting the airless qualities of this world.

Terry responds avidly both to the grandmother and to her home ('Oh, what a divine place! It's perfect', and later, 'I think I could stay here forever'). The stream of absolutes ('divine', 'perfect', 'forever') reveals a tendency towards idealisation and abstraction which characterises the grandmother as well. In conversation with Terry, she is disdainful of 'living, as they call it', which is her description of the mundane distractions that have kept her grandson from the practice of his art: 'Everything comes too easily to him. He's always attracted by the art he isn't practising, the place he hasn't been, the girl he hasn't met.' Although the grandmother advises Terry that

An Affair to Remember.
Terry hugs Nicky's
grandmother
(Cathleen Nesbitt).

she is too young for such a world ('. . . you have still to create your memories'), it is clear that all three of them feel a strong affinity for such a setting, and it is by seeing each other in juxtaposition with the grandmother that Terry and Nicky allow themselves to fall in love. Nevertheless, for the viewer of the film it is a morbid and cloyingly sentimental world, and there is something distastefully opportunistic in the way Terry runs back to embrace the grandmother as they leave, setting herself off to best advantage in Nicky's eyes – however unconscious her motivation – as he looks back at them both.

In setting up Nicky and Terry as the ideal romantic couple, the film offers us a number of parallels between them. For example, when Ken asks Terry, only half-jokingly, whether Nicky Ferrante was irresistible, after he has discovered that the famous ladies' man was a passenger on her ship, she agrees with his description; when, six months later, she prepares to meet Nicky as they'd arranged, she asks the woman in the dress shop for something that will make her 'irresistible' too. Similarly, each describes the other as 'sweet'. More interestingly, when Hathaway (Charles Watts) – a fellow passenger on board the ship – invites Nicky to join him and his wife and sister for a game of bridge, Nicky replies, 'Oh, I'm sorry, Mr Hathaway. But I cheat. It's an addiction'. A few moments later, as Terry is on her way to return Nicky's misplaced cigarette case to the purser, she tells him, 'I might as well confess. I am a jewel thief'. Not only do they make matching confessions, but they both reveal more than they realise. Nicky does cheat – if not at cards, then at love – and his 'addiction' to this is presumably part of his unending search for the ideal woman represented by his grandmother, not only in her excessive fidelity to his departed grandfather, but also, it would seem, in the unconditional love she showered on Nicky himself during his childhood. And Terry, a kept woman who, in her own words, is 'very fond of expensive things . . . furs and diamonds and stuff like that' may feel herself at some level to be a 'thief' and not the legitimate claimant to the clothes and jewels she so enjoys and which Ken supplies. Thus, the parallel evoked between them also represents a difference in terms of their respective histories and emotional needs.

Terry seeks respectability and a sense of self-worth, and Nicky's stated wish after their day in Villefranche ('I . . . I just want to be . . . worthy . . . of asking you to marry me', he tells her, his voice cracking) goes a long way towards fulfilling these needs; taking up her old job as a nightclub singer, which restores her self-sufficiency, does

An Affair to Remember.
Terry singing in the
Boston nightclub.

the rest. After the awkward uncertainties and hesitations of the shipboard romance and the sentimentality with which Terry sets herself off to advantage with the grand-mother (for example, at the piano, when she joins in singing the title song to the grandmother's accompaniment, but also elsewhere), the scenes of Terry at work are refreshingly straightforward: she never looks happier or more relaxed than in the Boston nightclub and as music teacher to the neighbourhood children, a job given to her by Father McGrath (Matt Moore) after her accident. In a sense, nothing more is required, and the film's resolution, when she is reunited with Nicky, is somewhat surplus to her needs, perhaps even at odds with them, since Nicky has made it clear that he wants to be her sole support.

Nicky's needs, on the other hand, have less to do with self-respect (though his becoming a successful breadwinner is the declared precondition of their satisfaction) than with a return to the childhood state of being unconditionally loved, as suggested earlier and as represented by the grandmother's world. The film offers us no per-spective on Nicky's mother, but the image of Nicky earning his living as a painter of advertising billboards, before his more serious artistic work has begun to sell, is rich in psychoanalytic possibilities. The first time we see Nicky with Courbet (Fortunio Bonanova), the benevolent gallery owner who encourages him in his work, Courbet advises Nicky to use his own name on his paintings in order to trade on his reputation as a famous womaniser rather than trusting to the quality of the work, but Nicky refuses ('The old Ferrante is dead'). From this scene, the film dissolves to a poster of Terry, and then to Terry herself, as she sings the song 'Tomorrowland' to a nightclub audience in Boston. Another dissolve, this time to Nicky on scaffolding in front of a beer advertisement showing a large image of a woman in a swimsuit, with Courbet, down below, telling Nicky the good news: 'I sold one of your women'. We fade out from Nicky, a small figure dominated by the much larger woman on the billboard, his head appearing to rest on her bosom as he leans back on the billboard and smiles at Courbet's words, and rejoin Terry singing the movie's title song (as she'd done, in French, in Villefranche) on her last night at work before her return to New York.

Nicky's claim that the old Ferrante is dead is ambiguous, of course: its ostensible implication is that the old Ferrante has developed into a new, more responsible adult version; but a more interesting reading is that the old Ferrante has in fact reverted to a younger version (that is, he has imaginatively returned to his childhood through

An Affair to Remember. Nicky leaning back on the billboard

his art). Though Nicky is unable to paint Terry accurately at this stage, as he had made clear in an earlier comment to Courbet ('Wouldn't you think that's the one thing I could remember?'), the stereotyped billboard image comes easily enough. The fact that our view of Nicky on the scaffolding occurs directly after Terry sings the suggestive lyrics of 'Tomorrowland' ('Close your eyes, make a wish, and you're there . . .') hints that what follows her song may be construed as a wish-fulfilment of sorts; given that the woman on the billboard dominates Nicky in size and position and given his smiles as he sinks back against her breast, it may be fruitful, further, to read the image as a displaced version of the mother who at some point and in some way has disappeared from his life. Courbet's comment that he has sold one of the female portraits delights Nicky, and the combination of the buying and selling of Nicky's 'women' with the demeaning use of a woman's image to sell beer suggests an apt symbolic revenge. Such a reading, however, is only speculative, in spite of the fact that it causes the various pieces of the sequence to fall satisfyingly into place and makes psychoanalytic sense. The moment is suggestive, no more than that, for Nicky's parents are a tantalising absence from his story, and his grandmother (with her self-sacrificing fidelity) swamps all other memories, even of Terry, except insofar as she is amalgamated with the grandmother in her reprise of the title song at the end of the sequence I've described. But perhaps, when Nicky's grandmother asked to speak to Terry alone in Villefranche, and Nicky commented, 'Please be kind,' his grandmother's reply – 'I won't betray you' – had a significance beyond its immediate context.

So in their time apart – the six months they agreed upon for Nicky to 'grow up' and become worthy of Terry – a more complicated process has taken place. The transformation of Nicky into a painter – a transformation into what he was before, as his grandmother makes clear – is both a growing up (to the extent that his paintings make money) and a turning back, through memory, to the past. According to Courbet, he only truly becomes a painter with the portrait of Terry and his grandmother, at a point when Terry seems lost to him forever after her accident and his grandmother is dead; the two women are thus linked and relegated to a romanticised imaginary landscape, his full possession of them in the painting making up for their actual loss. Terry, on the other hand, as I argued earlier, can both cherish the memory of Nicky's proposal as sufficient proof of her worthiness (after Ken's more cavalier appropriation of her as mistress through the controlling power of his wealth), while nonetheless enjoying the independence and self-sufficiency of her own return to work. Memories, for both of them, are a substitute for the presence of the person remembered; their precondition is absence, and a real relationship between Nicky and Terry ('living, as they call it') seems bound to disappoint them both. What is now clear, as they prepare to reunite, is the incompatibility of their needs: his enormous emotional neediness and her resistance, however unconscious, to being 'possessed' with such intensity, a resistance expressed in a number of ways, not least by the accident itself.

The first indication that Terry may not be as enthusiastic about the planned meeting with Nicky as she appears to be is the insufficient time she allows to shop for a new outfit immediately beforehand, even if one takes into account Ken's instructions to the saleswomen to delay her departure until he arrives (for she could easily have left at any time). The taxi driver's comment after she announces that she is going to get married – 'Marriage is something to rush to?' – is also telling, as are her half-delirious monologue in her hospital bed ('I know what I'm doing. I want my own way') and her subsequent stubborn refusal to let Nicky know what has happened. In a much earlier scene on board ship, Terry had warned a little boy, who had climbed up on some railings and got stuck, to be careful not to hurt himself:

> *Terry:* When I was little like you, I fell and I broke my leg.
> *Boy:* How is it now?
> *Terry:* Well, it's all right, I guess.
> *Boy:* Well, what're you crabbing about?
> *Terry:* I'm not cra . . . I'm sorry.

The film seems to be warning us, through this conversation, not to see Terry's accident, at the time of the planned meeting with Nicky, as anything to 'crab' about either. Certainly, Terry seems 'all right' this time too, in contrast to Nicky who is obviously misrepresenting his feelings when he responds to Courbet's comment that he can read Nicky's state of mind through his paintings: 'Broken heart? Oh, that stuff's not for me.' This denial of emotional distress by hiding it behind an un-convincing appearance of nonchalance is typical of many of Cary Grant's characters throughout his work in melodramatic films, for example, in *Only Angels Have Wings* (Howard Hawks, 1939), *Notorious* and others. His bitterness is most apparent after he and Terry meet by chance at the ballet, and he goes round to her apartment the next day.

I have emphasised the importance of certain fine details of performance in my account of *An Affair to Remember*, since it seems to me that it is in such gestures or in-flections – hesitations, eyes angrily narrowing, the spontaneity of a smile or look, the shy contrivance of a calculated pose – that much of the film's meaning is contained and re-vealed. Indeed, McCarey's work has been noted for the freshness of the performances he manages to elicit, and the credibility of the romance, as well as the suggestions of resistance to it, would be lost without such subtleties, even if viewers might not always be able to pinpoint the exact provenance of their impressions. Further, it is in the juxtaposition of one detail with another (the intimate warmth of Cary Grant's smile, say, against the nervous energy of his hands, or the clarity of Deborah Kerr's voice against the embarrassment betrayed by her lowered eyes) that much of the film's com-plexity is to be found. Although I have argued that Nicky and Terry are caught in an

An Affair to Remember. Photographs of Terry's and Nicky's shipboard romance.

intricate net of ideological and psychological cross-purposes, the performances of Grant and Kerr make us readily believe in their mutual affection and desire. And yet the film, like so many others, displays the extent to which desire is ill-served by the possibilities provided by a melodramatic narrative world.

Thus, through his internalised conviction that becoming a man involves being able to be the sole support of his wife, Nicky both suppresses his unresolved need to be a child and remains oblivious to Terry's need for self-respect through work of her own. Terry (in the wake of the relationship with Ken) is, in turn, unable to acknowledge openly her own fears of economic domination by yet another man, even if this is sanctified by marriage to a man she loves. Love is reduced, for both of them, to a universal state of frozen, but essentially unsustainable, perfection, despite the reminders McCarey provides throughout the film of the culturally mediated nature of romance: for example, in the various television broadcasts, including the interview with Nicky and Lois after his arrival in New York, which (wrongly) describes their relationship as 'their wonderful true-to-life romance', in the shipboard photographs taken of Nicky and Terry which convince their fellow passengers that they are together before their relationship has actually gone much beyond verbal sparring, and, of course, in Nicky's paintings. Nicky and Terry frequently try to catch each other off guard, thus:

> *Terry:* Yes, I'd like to meet your grandmother.
> *Nicky:* Well, you've got a date. Surprised?

> *Terry:* I'm beginning to think you *have* a grandmother . . .
> *Nicky:* Oh, *that's* surprising. I'll try to find her and prove it.

> *Nicky:* Tell me . . . uh . . . what have you two been talking about?
> *Terry:* Hmm . . . Oh, you'd be surprised.

Athough these exchanges betray a degree of uneasiness on the part of each of them with the conventional assumptions held by the other, which keep them on their guard in their scenes together, neither Terry nor Nicky ever explicitly disavows the ideological assumptions of the larger social world. One of the film's ironies, in fact, resides in the songs Terry teaches to the children in her charge, passing on ideologically normative ways of thinking (despite the fact that these have not always served her own best interests); one song advises them to follow a blatantly conventional moral code, while another makes a case for the very flights of fantasy that underpin her own views on romantic love, in preference to everyday life.

In the final scene of reconciliation in Terry's apartment, Nicky and Terry, now unable to read each other's thoughts as they claim they were able to before, try instead to read meaning into the other's words and demeanour. Terry rightly takes Nicky's gift to her of his grandmother's shawl as evidence of her death, and Nicky understands from the presence of his painting in her bedroom, given Courbet's description of the young woman to whom he gave it, that she is wheelchair-bound and unable to walk. The morbid and immobilising connotations of the grandmother's world and of the romance between Nicky and Terry, as represented by the shawl and by the painting of Terry and the grandmother together, are beyond doubt, and the passing on of the shawl to Terry locks her even more repressively into that world. In the earlier part of the scene, Nicky has described his wait on top of the Empire State Building as if he were the one who hadn't turned up, and Terry responds by taking on his role as the one who'd been left in the lurch. Nicky's attempt to express his pain, and Terry's efforts to understand it, are extremely moving, and seem to have a healing effect on Nicky, whose implied acceptance and forgiveness precede his discovery of the accident which kept Terry away. Nevertheless, this momentary exchange of identities is not enduring enough to overthrow the ideological requirements of a relationship made up of clearly differentiated roles and positionings. Terry's enforced immobility – despite her wishful thinking, we have no reason to think it isn't permanent – is an apt symbolic guarantee that she will never again either walk out on him or stand on her own two feet. From their embrace, we cut to the shot of bare trees in the snow which opened the film. Romantic melodrama, certainly.

The Courtship of Eddie's Father

Unlike *An Affair to Remember*, whose title suggests romantic melodrama, the title of *The Courtship of Eddie's Father* deliberately evokes romantic comedy, with its sly hint of impropriety, or at least of comic reversal (for courtship is meant to precede marriage and children), which, coupled with its openness in proclaiming such a reversal, reassure us of its innocence. It therefore seems unlikely that divorce or adultery on the part of the central male character will be the point here, so widowhood is implied, but this makes the 'Eddie' of the title a motherless child – a staple of melodramatic plotting. The mixed signals continue with the opening shot of the New York skyline, accompanied by initially energetic, then more romantically lush music, giving way to a brash satiric tone as we track in, while the seductive voice of a radio broadcaster, Norman Jones (Jerry van Dyke), addresses his audience – and New York City itself – as female: 'Wake up, Manhattan. Come out of that warm rosy dream. Open those big, luscious eyes and meet a new exciting day. I'm talking to you, ravishing, delicious, madcap girls still in that warm cosy bed. Now what you need is a nice hot cup of coffee, Bentley coffee, of course.' We see a coffee pot and a hand reaching to touch it and recoiling from the heat, as Norm continues: '. . . look out, don't burn those delicate sensuous fingers', and the camera readjusts its position to reveal that this 'female' listener is actually Tom Corbett (Glenn Ford), presumably the widower we've been anticipating, who, with his shirt unbuttoned at the neck and one sleeve partly rolled up, is busily trying to fry an egg.

The series of gender-based reversals linked by Norm's commentary and its (mis)-application to Tom, from the Manhattan skyline symbolic of the world of (male) business to the feminine sphere of domestic work to a reassertion of Tom's authority and power as he writes himself a note ('Stop Norm'), letting us know that he is, in fact, Norm's boss, alerts us to the interest the film is already beginning to show in subverting conventional expectations of how men and women ought to behave. Unlike *An Affair to Remember*, where the melodramatic opening shot of New York in the snow to the accompaniment of the title song is replaced by the subsequent un-romantic and comic television broadcasts which bring us down to earth, *The Courtship of Eddie's Father* provides an immediate and more intimate mix of melodrama and comedy. Tom's world teeters between the two, and many scenes veer from one to the other with little warning.

The intrusiveness of Norm's broadcast, which both invades Tom's domestic space and implicitly comments on his feminisation (his taking on the role of mother to his son), is echoed by the milkman who enters the kitchen uninvited, and Eddie (Ronny Howard) who gets into Tom's double bed during the night. In place of the 'ravishing, delicious, madcap girls still in that warm cosy bed', whom Norm had addressed over the airwaves, Tom finds not the endless romantic possibilities of Norm's fantasies, but his vulnerable son, Eddie. This is the film's first indication that Tom's relationships with the various women who will come into his life are to be less important, in emotional terms, than the growing closeness with his son. The transformation of the male, which, in films centred on romantic fresh starts, is typically wrought by the woman he loves, results here from losing his wife Helen and her place being taken by his son, rather than by another woman.

At first, Tom is ill at ease when admitting or expressing his emotions. Thus, when he drops Eddie off at school on his first day back after his mother's death, and Eddie asks if his mother is really dead, Tom's answer ('Yes, Eddie, she is') and Eddie's response ('Gosh . . . gosh') are immediately followed by the ringing of the school bell, which is both another intrusive interruption and a signal that Tom's emotions are dangerously near the surface. Variations upon this device occur at several points in the film. For example, when Elizabeth Marten (Shirley Jones) – his neighbour across the hall and his wife Helen's best friend – offers her condolences, and Tom begins to open up and talk, Eddie's screams over his dead goldfish provide an emotionally violent disruption (almost as though the boy's shrieks express the anger and pain Tom can't bring himself to reveal). I'll return later to this scene, as well as to other instances of Eddie's reactions standing in for Tom's. For the moment, it is worth noting that Eddie's question to Tom at school as to whether his mother is really dead follows his complaint that his shirt itches, and Tom's attempt at casual detachment in his answer: 'There's no reason for it to itch. It's one of your regular shirts. Matter of fact, that's the one that Mommy ironed.' The splashes of red around them in the clothes of some of the other children reinforce the sense of an emotional rawness which is not fully acknowledged in Tom's reply, and exemplify a common enough melodramatic strategy (as we saw in *Bigger than Life*, for example). This trace of the mother's presence from beyond the grave through the touch of the shirt on Eddie's body is an intensely physical one and, though the moment is superficially like Terry's inheritance of the shawl belonging to Nicky's dead grandmother in *An Affair to Remember*, it has a much warmer – less ghostly and repressive – feel to it, exposing the sense of loss shared by father and son and newly surfacing, strong emotional needs, rather than bearing the weight of symbolic resolution. The physicality of Tom's pain and anger – as he alternates between holding tight and letting go – is carried, above all, by Glenn Ford's remarkable performance.

Having dropped Eddie off at school, Tom goes in to work (again, it is the first time since Helen's death, and again the surroundings are accented with red) and, when greeted with outpourings of concerned sympathy on all sides, he appears uncomfortable and politely dismissive. Any feelings of loss at the death of his wife are transformed into anger at Norm for the excessive number of women he attracts. Both men – in terms of the ideological requirements of their broader social context – must be 'normalised': Tom, by finding an appropriate substitute for his dead wife, and Norm by shedding his surplus women and pairing off with just one. And yet the film seems not to be wholly in tune with these ostensible romantic projects, appearing both critical of Tom's puritanical attitude towards the good-natured Norm and, at the same time, sympathetic to Tom's own unfolding desire to develop a close relationship with Eddie rather than relinquishing the role of mother to someone else.

The goldfish scene brings many of these issues to a head. It is preceded by Eddie having a discussion with his father about the new housekeeper, Mrs Livingston (Roberta Sherwood), who will be arriving at any moment to look after them (an unthreatening relationship for Tom since it is an economic one, with no suggestion of an emotional commitment). Yet again, the accents of red in the decor emphasise Tom's – and Eddie's – continuing emotional fragility, though this is not particularly evident at first. Tom explains that the housekeeper is a 'sleep out':

Eddie: Sleep out?
Tom: Mmm hmm. Yeah, she sleeps out.
Eddie: Out where? Out of doors?
Tom: Wh . . . no, she sleeps out of *here*.
Eddie: Why? Are you mad at her?

While Eddie's comment is a humorous one, and the whole exchange reads almost like a double act with Tom playing straight man, it echoes Eddie's earlier question – 'Are you mad at me?' – when Tom had found the boy in his bed, the humour leading us straight back to the melodramatic. Eddie is quick to pick up on his father's unspoken anger, though he is uncertain as to precisely what has provoked it. Tentatively, Tom questions Eddie about what his teacher said on his first day back.

Eddie: About Mommy?
Tom: Yeah.
Eddie: She didn't say nothing.
Tom: Well, then, how do you know she knows?
Eddie: Oh, she kissed me and she looked at me and she let me pass out
all the papers – all that jazz.

Eddie's sensitivity to non-verbal meanings and oblique clues to other people's feelings continues throughout the film, most memorably in his later suspicions about Rita Behrens (Dina Merrill) and her relationship with his father: 'Skinny eyes and big bust is how you tell a bad lady from a good one,' he tells Tom, on the basis of his observations of women in comic books, when asking his father why he doesn't like the round-eyed Elizabeth the morning after she has nursed Eddie back to health.

But Eddie's astuteness in attributing significance to subtle aspects of expression, gesture and behaviour is also an indication of the ways in which we read films. As Victor Perkins points out, much of the meaning of the scene lies in the way Eddie's words about having wanted to cry at school are situated in a setting which unobtrusively emphasises his emotional fragility, as he and his father make a brave attempt at carrying on without Helen. As he takes a cup and saucer down from the cupboard, 'Eddie's precarious physical position on the stool, his careful handling of two fragile objects, counterpoint his attempt at emotional poise' (V.F. Perkins, *Film as Film: Understanding and Judging Movies*, Penguin, 1972, p.76). As Tom, clearly moved, is considering his reply, the doorbell rings and the housekeeper arrives, in a repetition of the device already cited whereby the expression of Tom's emotions is interrupted or frustrated by school bells, doorbells, telephone calls, and so on. The scene of Mrs Livingston's arrival, her meeting with Eddie and Tom, and her installation in the household dissolves to a shot of Tom coming home with the grocery shopping later in the evening of that same day. Shortly afterwards, their neighbour, Elizabeth, rings the bell, Mrs Livingston having already warned Tom against Elizabeth, a divorcée whom she sees as a 'floozie' out to get him. Tom's amusement at Mrs Livingston's outspokenness as he goes to open the door changes abruptly when he sees Elizabeth, who is a painful reminder of his wife. She explains that she's brought

The Courtship of Eddie's Father. Eddie (Ronny Howard), Elizabeth (Shirley Jones), Tom (Glenn Ford). Elizabeth brings fudge. Tom hugs Eddie.

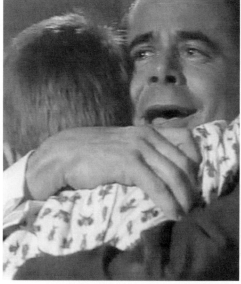

Eddie a plate of fudge with nuts, and her words – 'It's his favourite' – subtly imply that she knows things about his son that Tom does not. Elizabeth's unconscious attempt to establish a relationship with Eddie which excludes Tom is reinforced by the way she cuts Tom off as he tries to express what he felt on seeing her at the door, offering her services as a babysitter rather than meeting Tom's immediate need to be heard. Following her interruption, Tom shifts from sharing his feelings to denying them, insisting that he and Eddie are fine and getting back to normal. At this point, Eddie's scream over the dead goldfish both contradicts his words and gives rise to the anger that Tom can't express for himself. As Elizabeth takes over the process of calming Eddie down, suggesting to him that his screams have more to do with his mother than with the fish, Tom storms out angrily, pouring himself a drink. As in the first scene of the film (when Tom was preparing breakfast in a state of mild disarray), an even greater lack of tidiness conveys his troubled state of mind: after getting some ice, he leaves the refrigerator door open, drops an ice-cube on the living-room floor, spills liquor on the table and lifts the glass awkwardly by the rim.

As Elizabeth returns from Eddie's room, Tom's anger is unequivocal:

> *Tom:* A fish is a fish.
> *Elizabeth:* Tom!
> *Tom:* A fish is a fish, and his mother's his mother.
> *Elizabeth:* That isn't the point.
> *Tom:* He doesn't even care about those damn fish. I have to tell him to feed 'em half the time. It just takes about two seconds to give 'em a little feed.
> *Elizabeth:* He needed to cry, Tom.
> *Tom:* Well, let him cry according to the size of things.
> *Elizabeth:* It doesn't work that way.
> *Tom:* Well, I don't agree. Look, if you're sad, you cry. You don't save up your tears and go to a sad movie, do you?
> *Elizabeth:* But we do, we all do. Where do you think we get the tears we cry at a movie?

This seems to be the film's point of view asserting itself, through Elizabeth's words, offering a consideration of the processes of identification which allow melodramatic films to draw on the experiences and emotions of their viewers. But, if Elizabeth's words are therefore privileged over Tom's, which are seen to be self-deceived, our sympathies are nevertheless much more firmly with Tom. In any case, he seems to be aware enough that Eddie was not crying for the fish ('He doesn't even care about those damn fish . . .'). Indeed, later in the film when Eddie has run away from summer camp, Tom's glance at the goldfish is poignant because they remind him of his missing son and thus intensify his anguish. At this stage, however, although Eddie's screams have released Tom to express his own anger and direct it against Elizabeth, where it belongs, both for her refusal to listen to him and her attempt to take over the mothering role with Eddie (unlike the scene of Tom at work where his anger at Norm seemed misdirected, no other more appropriate 'target' being readily to hand), he is, nevertheless, unable to express the real reasons for his outburst, presenting it as anger at Elizabeth's suggestion that Eddie was thinking of Helen when he screamed.

The final and most moving part of the scene takes place after Elizabeth has rushed out and Tom has retreated to his bedroom, with its cold shades of grey and blue, his anger spent, looking round at the various reminders of his wife as Eddie comes in.

> *Eddie:* I know, Dad. I know how much you miss Mommy. [*He runs to Tom and they hug throughout the rest of the scene.*]
> *Tom:* I'm glad you know, Eddie. Now it's something that we know about each other. Of course, I . . . *we* miss Mommy . . . and . . . very much, and we will for a long time.
> *Eddie:* How long does it take, Dad?
> *Tom:* Well, let me put it this way, Eddie. No matter *how* long it takes, we're going to be all right. Just as long as I can tell you everything that I feel and you can tell me.
> *Eddie:* Everything?
> *Tom:* Everything.
> *Eddie:* Always?
> *Tom:* Always. I tell you what, let's you and I have a . . . sort of a secret pact, just between us.
> *Eddie:* Okay, Dad.
> *Tom:* Oh, Eddie.

The contrast with the earlier part of the scene is striking. In the privacy of the bedroom, Tom finds a secret space where he and his son can express their emotional needs openly, without any need for defensiveness or evasive stratagems. Eddie's innocence of the requirements of adult masculinity – his much greater dependence on body language in interpreting how people feel – accounts for the ease with which he can accept his father in his mother's place, responding directly to his own needs and to those of his father. The spontaneity Eddie shows when he runs to hug his father contrasts with Tom's earlier defensiveness with Elizabeth when his arms were folded tightly against his body.

This scene, with its essentially melodramatic concerns about the difficulties men have in openly expressing their emotions, dissolves to a much more comedic one, as we join Eddie and Tom coming out of a Western, Eddie insisting that 'they cheat with the horses' depending on whether the film makers want the good guys or the bad guys to get away. As they stop for a game in a penny arcade, they're approached by the gaudily attractive Dollye Daly (Stella Stevens), who asks Tom if she can 'borrow' his son, as a protection against 'mashers' while she's posing to have her portrait painted on a tie to send to her father back home in Montana. She's in New York to learn confidence and poise: 'I'm supposed to do one thing every day that I'm afraid to do but I really want to do.' In response to Eddie's suggestion to his father in the taxi on the way home that Dollye may be lonely, Tom agrees to help her if he can, which he does by introducing her to Norm in the following scene at work, having decided that, contrary to appearances, she is no 'floozie'.

Dollye's unfolding relationship with Norm provides a comic counterpoint to Elizabeth's eventual relationship with Tom. Mrs Livingston's initial description of Elizabeth as a floozie is matched by Eddie's question to Tom about whether Dollye is a floozie ('No, I don't think so. No, I . . . I . . . I don't think so at all'); Elizabeth's status as a divorcée and Dollye's blatantly sexual appearance have opened them both up to suspicion. Both women resist such conventional judgments of themselves, and their efforts at moral self-improvement (Elizabeth's job as a volunteer nurse, Dollye's classes in confidence-building and poise) are based on a common need for respect; Dollye, especially, reveals aspects of herself which defy our expectations, like her skill on the drums, and this is echoed in the scene where Elizabeth plays the bongos while Mrs Livingston and Eddie dance. Most importantly, Dollye's innocent request to 'borrow' Eddie from Tom meets its melodramatic match in the less explicit way Elizabeth moves in on Eddie to the exclusion of Tom. Dollye's comment to Norm that others – presumably including Norm himself – may be just as insecure as she, is indirectly confirmed by Norm when he advises her to fake self-confidence, to adopt it as a kind of façade. Tom and Elizabeth, Dollye and Norm, are all constrained by the conventional roles other people expect them to play (as widower, divorcée, floozie and womaniser respectively), yet each appears unsure beneath the surface bravado, though, in Dollye's case, the insecurity is openly and cheerfully acknowledged. Thus, it seems that the kind of material that tends to remain implicit (or symbolic) in melodrama can become explicit in comedy, where a more light-hearted treatment renders it safe.

That Tom chooses Rita over Elizabeth is understandable since, unlike Elizabeth, Rita shows little interest in mothering Eddie – her token efforts, as her relationship with Tom becomes more serious, meet with little success – and she is never seen in Tom's apartment. This contrasts dramatically with Tom's relationship with Elizabeth, who frequently invades his domestic space. Tom, on the other hand, never enters Elizabeth's apartment at all, though he is seen on more than one occasion in Rita's. It appears that, in his relationship with Rita, Tom prefers, like Mrs Livingston, to 'sleep out'. Elizabeth consistently makes Tom angry, and his emotions are very near the surface in their scenes together, whereas he seems to slip into a much easier, more conventionally masculine role in the scenes with Rita, which have a coolness suggesting emotional disengagement, despite his claims to the contrary. He can thus adopt a confident guise of suave masculinity with Rita (for example, in the scenes of them dancing together when Eddie is away at summer camp), based on ideologically familiar scripts, while nonetheless preserving a private space, excluding Rita, where he and Eddie can be together and his deeper emotional needs can be expressed and met. The relationship with Rita is thus little more than a convenient front for his relationship with his son. So, when the relationship with Eddie begins to unravel because of Eddie's and Rita's mutual lack of affection, it is clear who has to go.

The breaking point comes after Tom has told Eddie, on a visit to his son at camp, that he intends to marry Rita: 'All right, now let's get this one thing straight. You're a boy and I'm a man. When you grow up you'll live your life. I live my life. That's what a man's supposed to do.' We dissolve from this scene to a shot of Rita's poodle, as Rita and Tom come in to her apartment and he proposes. After Rita announces to Tom that she thinks it would be best to send Eddie away to his uncle for a while, her poodle growls, and the telephone rings, with the news that Eddie has run away. In narrative terms, Eddie's decision to run off has its motive in Tom's decision to marry Rita. But the way it follows on from Rita's revelation that she intends to send Eddie away (which Eddie obviously doesn't hear) implies that, more symbolically, it is a reaction to her present words, perhaps even an enactment of Tom's desire to break off with Rita as a result, the intrusive telephone call yet another example of Tom's emotional reaction being hijacked by events offscreen as his feelings are displaced onto and enacted by his son.

Meanwhile, Elizabeth's appropriation of Eddie has continued to escalate. Shortly after Rita has made her first appearance, Eddie comes into the living-room – a small, shivering figure – where his father is watching a romantic scene from *Mogambo* on television (his emotional involvement in the onscreen kiss belying his earlier denial to Elizabeth that our reactions to movies are anything to do with the feelings we have about events in our own lives). Panicky about Eddie's illness, he rushes across the hall to Elizabeth's apartment and asks her to help. She calms him down and, once again, as in the scene with the fudge, uses her privileged knowledge (here, as a volunteer nurse) to dismiss him – 'Tom, go to bed, please' – and care for Eddie herself. Unwillingly, he goes to his room (just as he did after their argument about the fish and her departure), looking at a photo of Eddie and his mother together which, like the scenario taking place in Eddie's room nearby, also excludes him. In the morning, Tom offers to pay Elizabeth for her help, and another angry departure ensues, followed by another emotional discussion between father and son, where Eddie again helps his father to come to terms with his mother's death, Tom struggling to contain his emotions as Eddie describes how Helen told him to be a good boy and to take care of his father.

> *Eddie:* Did you know that, Dad?
> *Tom:* [*unable to speak, his lips pressed tightly together as he struggles to contain his emotions, before he soundlessly mouths the answer*] No.

Of course, the fact that, as he describes his mother being wheeled away to the hospital, Eddie is lying in bed after his own illness, gives an added resonance to the scene, as Tom is forced to contemplate – at least momentarily – the possibility of losing his son as well.

Following Tom's proposal to Rita, when Eddie runs away from summer camp, it is to Elizabeth that Eddie returns. This final example of Elizabeth's occupation in Eddie's life of the place Tom wants for himself provokes his most bitterly aggressive, and yet most emotionally vulnerable, attack on Elizabeth's good intentions. The inarticulate jumble of his words and the rumpled appearance of his clothes, after the long night searching for Eddie, reinforce the impression that he has no more reserves to fall back on, having been cast adrift from those ready, but emotionally dead, forms of masculinity which the relationship with Rita had provided: 'Look, will you please let *me* think about Eddie for a change? He is *my* son, isn't he? Everybody knocking him back and forth, bouncing him back and forth, all this to get to *me*, to get to me . . . ' At last, Tom is directing his anger not just at the appropriate person, but for the appropriate reasons as well, though his mode of expression is still confused. His feeling of beleaguerment and of raw emotional need are clear enough, however, and issue forth in an attack on Elizabeth at her most vulnerable point – 'Oh, I can see how your marriage *had* to fail' – an accusation which typecasts her again, as Mrs Livingston had done at first, as the bad divorcée. She slaps his face, refusing to apologise, and runs off once again.

The Courtship of Eddie's Father. A dishevelled
Tom directs his anger at Elizabeth.

With a certain inevitability by this point, the pattern of earlier scenes continues
to its final stage, as Elizabeth sends Eddie back across the hall to his father, and
Tom expresses his feelings to his son, both of them near tears.

> *Tom:* Ed . . . Eddie, do you . . . do you know what you put me through?
> *Eddie:* Yeah.
> *Tom:* I wonder . . . You know, *you* are the most important thing in the
> world to me, Eddie. If anything should ever happen to you and if I
> didn't know where you were for a day or a week, I don't know what I'd
> d . . . I'd do.
> *Eddie:* I guess I didn't think.
> *Tom:* Well, I guess you didn't.
> *Eddie:* But I won't do it again. I won't ever leave you again, Dad. I won't
> even go back to camp unless you want me to. I'll stay right here with you.

Whereas their earlier discussions centred on their shared loss of Helen, they now
more directly express their love for each other. In Tom's relationships with women,
nothing has the intensity of this scene with his son. As with other instances of concentrated emotion in the film, this one too is interrupted – by a phone call from
Rita. Tom tells her that he needs to spend more time with Eddie – 'You see he's
very disturbed at the moment . . .' – though his words are much more applicable to
his own state of mind than to that of his son.

One of the many merits of the film is the clear-sightedness with which it juxtaposes
Tom's partial recognition of his emotional neediness with the conventional wisdom
he so often falls back on when advising Eddie. In the privacy of their secret pact, he
can confide to him that everything will be fine 'just as long as I can tell you everything that I feel and you can tell me'. However, in explaining his reasons for wanting
to marry Rita, all he can appeal to is a vague conception of male duty: '. . . I live my
life. *That's what a man's supposed to do . . .*' [my italics]. He is caught between wanting
to mother Eddie and trying to be a conventional man, though unconsciously resisting
full capitulation by preferring a woman like Rita who will not intrude on his private
space with Eddie, at least until she suggests that they send Eddie away. Eddie
himself is more able than his father to see through Rita's token expressions of good
will: 'Listen, I don't like Rita, Dad. She butts in. Don't you like Elizabeth?' So, while
Elizabeth disturbs the closeness between father and son by her affection for the

son, Rita turns out to be even more disruptive by wishing to remove Eddie from the picture altogether.

Despite Eddie's sharper instincts, at least where Rita is concerned, the film shows us the processes that can cause a boy like Eddie to grow up to be a man like Tom – through absorbing ideas about masculinity gleaned from comics, television and movies, as well as from his elders. For example, Eddie tells Elizabeth that brave boys don't bleed when they're cut, and she gets him to return to his father by reminding him, 'You think Chester would run out on Matt Dillon?' Similarly, Tom falls back on clichés like, 'That's what a man's supposed to do', or on generalisations such as 'Women *like* that, Eddie. It pleases them" when advising Eddie to give his friend Cherry something of his own as a gift, instead of money, despite his own earlier attempt to pay Elizabeth for looking after Eddie when he was ill. So Tom is full of contradictory tendencies, and the freshness of Eddie's ideas about the world depends upon the extent to which he still hasn't fully grasped the rules of how to be a man, although he's learning fast. Thus, he is able to find a fat girl beautiful, but already knows that he has to prepare his father not to act surprised when he meets her; the earlier scene on New Year's Eve, when Eddie learns about women's measurements from a magazine article he's reading about Jayne Mansfield and asks his father how much a woman should 'dent in' at the waist, is already preparing him to reject girls like Cherry in the future. Indeed, his anger at Cherry, after his father has told Eddie of his plan to marry Rita ('Hi, Eddie. Gee, your father's nice. I like him a whole lot.' 'Aw, shut up!'), is similar to the anger Tom expresses towards Elizabeth whenever his emotional needs are blocked.

The Courtship of Eddie's Father, like *An Affair to Remember*, dramatises the mismatch between the characters' desires and received wisdom about how men and women are supposed to behave. Normative behaviour is shown to mask opposing feelings and desires. Thus, Norm advises Dollye to fake self-confidence, and, in the restaurant scene with Rita, Tom tells Eddie to 'act like you're enjoying yourself'. Tom's anger – to an extent like Eddie's in the scene with Cherry – is a sign of his resistance to the frustration of his emotional needs, and Elizabeth's anger, after Tom blames her for the failure of her marriage ('How did she get that mad?' Eddie wonders), is at least partly to do with a refusal to be typecast as a bad divorcée. Thus, again as in *An Affair to Remember*, the male desire to acknowledge and express his emotional neediness is met by the female desire to be respected and not to be perceived through the demeaning stereotypical roles of mistress (Terry) or of divorcée (Elizabeth). It is instructive, as well as amusing, that Eddie imagines his parents to have been engaged in discussions when they retreated to their bedroom and closed the door, since honest communication between men and women is continually seen to be thwarted by the conflict between desires and social roles. It is as if men and women have learned the wrong language to communicate their desires, like Mrs Livingston, who has studied Spanish before setting off to visit her daughter and South American son-in-law in Brazil, only to discover that the national language there is Portuguese. In learning the language of being a man, Tom is left without an easy way to communicate his desire to be a 'mother' to his son.

The film ends with a reconciliation between Elizabeth and Tom, orchestrated by Eddie, who acts almost as director of the final scene, standing in the space between

The Courtship of Eddie's Father. Eddie in the hall at the end of the film.

their two apartments as they talk on the telephone. It is an ambiguous ending, following on from the courtship rehearsal that Eddie gets his father to enact with him: 'Please, Dad. We'll make believe I'm Elizabeth, and you be you.' Like Nicky's reversal of roles with Terry near the end of *An Affair to Remember*, when he pretends he's the one who missed their appointment at the top of the Empire State Building, Eddie too takes on a female role, but he can only imagine it in stereotypical terms (for example, addressing Tom as 'my future husband' and 'my sugar-man'). We are left wondering whether Elizabeth will continue to invade Tom's life and space and edge him out of his close relationship with Eddie, or – as suggested by Eddie's position in the intervening space between the two apartments and by the smiles and relaxed postures of Tom and Elizabeth as they talk – whether they will be able to open up an emotional space large enough for all three of them to inhabit together. The film seems both to recognise the limited room for manoeuvre in a repressive melodramatic world and to give us a glimpse of the possibilities – at least through the artifice of film – of a more open, comedic outcome.

The Tamarind Seed

So far, a central issue that has emerged in the examination of romantic new beginnings has been the extent to which romances embedded within melodramatic narrative worlds are able to offer an escape from their repressiveness. *An Affair to Remember* was seen to edge its romantic couple into a space where time stands still (life replaced by remembering and vitality giving way to immobility), its couple unable to allow themselves to think of alternatives to the traditional roles of male breadwinner and dependent wife, despite suppressed desires to do so, as evinced by details of performance (such as Terry's exuberance and well-being in the scenes of her at work), dialogue ('Marriage is something to rush to?') and symbolism (for example, the view of Nicky smiling and leaning back against the bosom of the towering woman on the billboard behind him). *The Courtship of Eddie's Father*, on the other hand, a film with strong comedic as well as melodramatic elements, is more promising in the way it allows Tom to develop as he increasingly opens up emotionally to his son, though the romance with Elizabeth, at least initially, is an obvious threat to this release. Our sense of expanding possibilities is fuelled by Tom's growing appropriation of his dead wife's place and by the 'romance' with Eddie, rather than by the traditional romance with the girl-next-door. So neither film offers heterosexual romance as a clear way forward. In the case of *The Tamarind Seed*, I should like to examine the same concerns: to what extent does the romantic reunion of Feodor Sverdlov (Omar Sharif) and Judith Farrow (Julie Andrews), at the end of the film, provide an escape from the vicious web of political intrigue and conflicting ideological allegiances in which, until then, they've been caught?

As in *An Affair to Remember*, the romantic couple first meet while on holiday, and in both cases they are closely watched by others around them. However, whereas the interest taken in Nicky's and Terry's shipboard romance by their fellow passengers in McCarey's film is essentially benevolent, Feodor and Judith are observed with secrecy and malicious intent by the agents of their respective governments. There is no question but that the world of espionage depicted in this film is a thoroughly nasty and invasive one, contaminating all of the narrative spaces within the film. In the process, the British are implicated as completely and as critically as the Russians on the other side, the film providing counterparts across the ideological divide for many of the central characters. Thus, General Golitsyn (Oscar Homolka) is paralleled by Jack Loder (Anthony Quayle), each of them manipulating others with cold, but smug, calculation. The distaste with which various British characters comment on Loder – 'Oh, that frightful man', 'I don't like that man', 'that monster Loder' – informs our reaction not just to Loder but also to Golitsyn, whom we first see in grotesque close-up at the Embassy party as he steps in front of Loder and George MacLeod (Bryan Marshall) – a moment bracketed, more or less, by the first two of the critical comments about Loder just cited. The antipathy to Loder seems to be based partly on class (his working-class accent positioning him in clear contrast to those around him), and our antipathy to Golitsyn is as much a reaction to his coarse and unappealing physical appearance as to his behaviour. However, the fact that all three comments on Loder are made by women – Margaret Stephenson (Sylvia Syms), Rachel Paterson (Celia Bannerman) and Judith Farrow, respectively – suggests that Loder's monstrousness to women, and the monstrousness to women of the high-powered world of espionage which he represents, are to be issues of particular interest in the film.

The undermining of ideological difference is insisted upon from its first apparent display through the use of opposing symbolic colours in the credit sequence. The movie begins with a close-up of a blue eye in a blue face (the only use of blue in the sequence), which, as the camera tracks out, is shown to be Judith Farrow's. Feodor Sverdlov's face, washed in red, appears a moment later on the left of the screen, turning to watch Judith as she recedes into the distance and disappears. However, there is nothing naturalistic in the way his face turns smoothly towards her, a movement suggesting not so much human agency as a manipulation of images by a controlling force elsewhere. The dreamscape of the credits is far from a depiction of real narrative events in real narrative time and space, but its imagery offers us a number of tentative conclusions which will be developed at later points in the film. First, the blue/red contrast between Judith and Feodor, initially implying a clear-cut British/Russian divide (the true blue capitalist versus the Communist red) is more apparent than real, or, at least, will be transgressed in the course of the film, perhaps by romance, if we consider the way Feodor emerges, at one point in the credits, from the empty space behind Judith's silhouette, where no figure or point of entry was visible before, hinting at a confluence of identities of some sort. However, the fact that the red is increasingly associated with Judith, as well as Feodor, suggests not so much her possible defection to Russia in the course of the film (how could it, with Julie Andrews in the role?) as another agenda altogether. The red flames and smoke that provide the background to Judith's figure in one of the early shots are later revealed to be memories of her husband's death by burning, in a car crash, or, rather, her imagination reworking the event, for nothing in the film's narrative suggests that she was present.

The sequence ends inside Feodor's mind, as it were, with the camera moving quickly forward into the silhouette of his head, as the area within its outline dissolves to a shot of waves on the beach in Barbados, thus implicating his fantasies, too, in the narrative which follows. Their fantasies mesh in a shared sense of complicity in a guilty world (whether that of espionage or of a loveless marriage where her husband's death can be seen as the realisation of Judith's guilty wish to be rid of him). The tree near their adjacent bungalows, which, Feodor warns Judith, reportedly drips poison on those who stand beneath it in the rain, seems an apt symbol for the corrosive atmosphere in which they are immersed. By contrast, in the course of an excursion to the Bridgetown Museum, they read about the tamarind tree, whose seeds in the shape of a man's head – two of which are displayed in the glass-covered case in the museum – are said to proclaim the innocence of a slave who was unjustly hanged from its branches after being accused of the theft of a sheep. Whereas Feodor sees Judith as a sentimentalist ('You believe in innocent slaves and miraculous tamarind seeds'), he insists, 'There is no tamarind tree. There was no innocent slave. There is no force outside this world which gives justice to the weak. There is nothing but man . . .' It is perhaps worth underlining the irony that Judith's dream of innocence – her eager acceptance of the legend of the tamarind seed – is a vision of innocence not rewarded, but enslaved and punished, and vindicated only after death.

After the dream-like imagery of the credit sequence, the rest of the film until the final reunion in Canada is largely structured around the repetition of a single insistent pattern of cuts and overlapping dialogue. Over and over again, we cut from a given scene to another whose separateness – both spatially and in terms of characters – is both sharply defined by the cut and yet contradicted by the fact that the dialogue of one scene overlaps with the images of the other. Through the soundtrack, in other words, the world of spying and intrigue consistently bleeds into the more private space of various characters who don't always realise they are under surveillance or being discussed and who, in turn, are themselves often shown to be prying and speculating about others. The emphasis on surveillance, distrust and betrayal which runs through the film, as well as the symbolically weighted image of the poisonous tree, suggest that none of the characters – including the two vacationers in Barbados – can find shelter from the corrosive atmosphere infecting political and sexual relationships alike in the world of the film. Similarly, through the overlapping dialogue between scenes, the integrity of the shot itself is undermined as words from one shot infiltrate the space of another.

Although many of the characters are presented as intelligent and emotionally complex, their motives are often hidden behind impenetrable surfaces. The problem for us, as viewers, of how to read the characters and their motives is foregrounded in numerous ways, for example, in an image of Golitsyn standing in front of a screen

The Tamarind Seed.
Golitsyn (Oscar
Homolka) offering
himself to be 'read'.

on which a document is projected, the words appearing to be written across his face as if we're simultaneously being invited to 'read' him, yet are being thwarted in any such attempt by the opaque surface he presents, the film giving us little sense of what he thinks or feels. Similarly the loving inscription from Margaret Stephenson to her husband Fergus (Daniel O'Herlihy), a high-ranking British diplomat, on the cigarette lighter he's inadvertently left at home appears to reveal the state of their relationship, but is actually misleading. In addition, the lighter, which is also a camera, conceals the fact that Fergus is a spy for the Russians, although the game is given away to Margaret precisely because she knows the inscription's sentiments to be false and not written by her: 'Since I haven't loved you for years, and I didn't give it to you in the first place, I was naturally rather curious.' Thus, in the cases of Golitsyn and Fergus alike, the exteriors they present to the world prove to be either opaque or misleading. The difficulties presented by the film's surface world are particularly urgent for us where Feodor is concerned; the film offers us enigmatic and shadowy close-ups of him at various points which are clearly intended to make us question

The Tamarind Seed. The inscription on the cigarette lighter.

whether he can be trusted (for example, when he sees Judith off to the airport on Barbados, or when he dines out with her in London after her return home).

The sequence in the restaurant in London where Feodor and Judith dine together is preceded by Feodor discussing Judith with Golitsyn, assuring him, 'I believe that I will be able to recruit her'. This is a truly wrenching moment for the audience, since, despite the pervasive sense that no one can be trusted, we had come to trust Feodor and his romantic intentions; the disillusionment of what appears a calculated betrayal of Judith's trust (and ours) is a bitter one. The way his conversation with Golitsyn lingers on the soundtrack, in an instance of the familiar pattern, over the shot of Judith coming out of the Home Office, where she works, to meet him, increases our unease. It is ironic, then, that he regains our confidence – telling Judith that he won't try to recruit her, 'though I *have* told my own people that I would do this' – only moments before Judith goes on to remind him of his boast that he can 'lie like a trooper', and only moments after he has told her what a bad interrogator she would make: 'You stare into my eyes to see if I'm lying, but people can lie with their eyes.' Not for the first or the last time, Judith's gullibility is paralleled by our own, as we readily abandon the sinking feeling that Feodor has betrayed her for the reassurance – based on nothing more solid than Feodor's say-so – that he has not. Towards the end of the film, we share Judith's belief that Feodor is dead, and discover at the same time as she does that he is actually alive. Despite the many lessons the film offers us to the effect that appearances mislead – in Loder's cynical words, 'No-one's to be trusted, nothing is to be believed, and anyone is capable of doing anything' – we continue to take the narrative at face value. Thus, even as we discard impressions which have proved to be false (that Feodor can't be trusted; that he's dead), we eagerly latch on to others with equal confidence (that he can be trusted after all; that he's really alive).

Our gullibility, the ease with which we're led, is most interestingly deployed in the sequence at the airport, when Loder's man, MacLeod, outwits the Russian who is tailing Feodor by planting a fake gun on him so that Feodor and Judith can make their escape while the Russian is detained by airport security. The airport sequence provides us with a great deal of pleasure in the temporary restoration of a conventional world of moral certainties, where good can be not only easily distinguished from bad – at least now that Feodor has come over to the British side – but expected to defeat it. In a world where both sides have been shown to be equally nasty and manipulative in the tactics they use, we are nonetheless encouraged by the prospect of narrative pleasure to suspend this knowledge for the sake of a good chase and the pleasures of identifying with the would-be lovers in their anticipated escape. Our confidence is paralleled by that of the normally cynical Feodor as he tells Judith, 'Barbados is British; Mr Loder will be able to protect me there'. However, in both our case and theirs, this trust will be seen to be badly misplaced when Judith is burned in the explosion and Feodor is apparently killed. Even when it emerges that Feodor is alive, this turns out to have been more a matter of chance than of British reliability, since he is saved only by the lucky timing of Judith's worried telephone call to MacLeod when Feodor refuses to stay 'safely' indoors, as advised, and is removed from the bungalow with only seconds to spare before the blast. (This moment has its equivalent in *The Searchers*, when Debbie, played as a child by Lana Wood, is sent out of the house where her family have barricaded themselves against an imminent Comanche attack and is the only one to survive. Thus, Ethan's earlier advice to his brother to 'stay close' – like Loder's advice to Feodor to stay under cover – is turned into a virtual death sentence.)

Douglas Pye's account of Fritz Lang's *Beyond a Reasonable Doubt* (1956) may be relevant to our appetite for straightforward narrative pleasures in *The Tamarind Seed* when he describes the viewer of Lang's film as 'confronted by the challenge of appearances and thrown back on habitual forms of reading and response' ('Film Noir and Suppressive Narrative: Beyond a Reasonable Doubt' in ed. Cameron, *The Movie Book of Film Noir*, 1992). However, Pye is concerned with Lang's film as an example of suppressive narrative, which is not precisely what is happening in the Edwards film. Of course, to some extent, all films hold something back, at least initially. Thus:

> This restriction of access to reliable information about motive and character is built on the basic conditions of film as a dramatic art. In its more straightforward form, it can also be associated with the other forms of narrative suppression which characterise the crime story and which form part of the expectations we are likely to bring to our viewing of *film noir* . . . it is the extension of this challenge to the spectator's wider relationship to the narrative and the role played by massively suppressive narrative that are particularly remarkable in Fritz Lang's *Beyond a Reasonable Doubt* (1956). (p.100)

In the course of Lang's film, although there are many clues to the truth, they are noticeable only retrospectively – 'On initial viewing, in fact, they may hardly appear as signifiers at all . . .' (Cameron 1992, p.107) – and it is only through a final revelation of the truth that we are able to understand the film's events in a new light.

In contrast, the enigmatic images of Feodor not only come across as heavy with significance the first time one sees them, but they remain enigmatic on subsequent viewings, any access to their meaning continuing to be blocked. If *Beyond a Reasonable Doubt* concludes by revealing the ways in which we allow ourselves to be led to a false reading of motives and events, *The Tamarind Seed*, while frequently presenting its surface world as unreliable, fails to offer any revelatory key to unlocking an essentially unknowable – or, in any case, blocked – world of human motivation beyond this. That Feodor is not out to recruit Judith does little to establish what his true motives are, especially as his first romantic approach to her occurs before they've met or spoken. As a married man, is he simply interested in a superficial fling with a woman whose appearance pleases him? Is he already aware of the possibility that he may need to come over to the West for his own safety, thus choosing an attractive English woman either to help him or to accompany him into exile? There is simply no way of telling. Similarly, the news that Feodor is still alive at the end of the film (which has been suppressed for only a few minutes of screen time) does nothing to elucidate what has gone before, but comes across as an arbitrary outcome with no epistemological significance, unlike Lang's revelations, which retrospectively make sense of an entire film.

If *Beyond a Reasonable Doubt* requires a retrospective reading of the film in the light of what we have learned about film rhetoric and its powers to deceive us, then *Schindler's List* (as we saw in Chapter Two) requires us, in the light of the Holocaust, to read the world anew; in the aftermath of Auschwitz, both language and the ordinary appearances of the world were shown to have been irrevocably transformed, rendering innocent readings obsolete. In *The Tamarind Seed*, in contrast, the words and surfaces of the world have been either converted to unreadable, mocking images, like the words superimposed on Golitsyn's face, or reduced to inert factual descriptions of the world. We can make out the words of the document before Golitsyn moves in front of the screen, but they become indecipherable once they appear on his face, and, in any case, they tell us nothing of Golitsyn himself. Our difficulties are mirrored by those of the characters within the narrative. Thus, the spies who report on Feodor's and Judith's comings and goings are at a loss as to how to interpret the merely factual evidence they compile. For example, in discussing Feodor's relationship with Judith, Loder tells his colleagues, 'Maybe it's just a coincidence . . . and maybe not,' and he later comments to Fergus about Judith having met Captain Richard Paterson (David Baron) a few years after her husband's death, 'Well, knowing the gallant Group Captain, it's not hard to guess what happened.' Such talk is little more than speculation, as Loder's words – 'Maybe . . . maybe not', 'not hard to guess' – make clear. The material assembled by both sides resists their attempts to draw conclusions from appearances alone, and they are able to do little more than to report the appearances themselves (a state of affairs which very nearly has fatal consequences for Feodor and Judith later in the film, when they are under Loder's protection, though Golitsyn's people turn out to be just as fallible to the point of being comically inept).

The opacity of words and images which mean nothing beyond themselves is explicitly addressed in the scene in the restaurant when Judith reminds Feodor that he has boasted he 'can lie like a trooper'. When he asks her what this means, she replies, 'Oh, it's just an expression. It doesn't mean anything, really.' The exchange is echoed by two others at the nightclub later that night, when Feodor asks Judith the meaning of the expression 'true blue', and Judith asks Sandy Mitchell (Sharon Duce), the English girlfriend of Feodor's friend Dimitri Memenov (Constantin De Goguel), what the Russian word *truba* (chimney) means. The links through sound between the three expressions – trooper – *truba* – true blue – may alert us to their non-semantic dimension in the film. When Judith and Feodor are back in Barbados in the course of his defection, he makes the mistake of trying to ascribe meaning to a song which is playing on the radio and to which they danced in the nightclub by telling Judith that, 'It's a good omen' only minutes before the bungalow blows up. Judith's attempt to attribute meaning to the tamarind seed is a further example of misplaced sentimentality, which, by the end of the film, is thoroughly discredited.

The two instances when Feodor gives Judith a tamarind seed, in both cases in a white envelope to be opened in his absence, represent a move from Judith's belief in divine justice to Feodor's in an uncaring fate. The first occasion is when Feodor gives Judith the envelope to open on her flight home from the holiday in Barbados. Though the existence of the tamarind seed he gives her might seem to vindicate her belief in the legend of the innocent slave (Judith herself certainly seems to think so, having declared earlier, 'I *want* one of those seeds. Just to prove something to you'), it of course does nothing of the kind. They'd already seen such seeds in the Bridgetown Museum, and their existence was never in question, only their meaning, which remains opaque. What we have, rather, is an act of romantic gallantry on Feodor's part, an indulgence in the fantasy for her sake (and indirectly for his own, perhaps, as part of a strategy of seduction), with Feodor himself being at one remove from the illusion of a universe that makes sense in moral terms. It is a lighter version of the heart-rending moment in *It's a Wonderful Life* when George Bailey pretends to paste the petals back on his young daughter's rose, restoring her faith in miracles just when he is himself on the edge of despair.

The second time Judith receives a tamarind seed from Feodor is via Loder at the convalescent home, when she thinks that Feodor is dead. Her physical scars from the explosion are emblematic of her disillusioned state – her loss of faith in the ideological platitudes that kept her going earlier on – and the seed now carries no connotations beyond the simple fact that Feodor is alive. That is, the significance of the seed he gives her is simply the fact that he's given it to her. Thus, it is a confirmation of his own earlier claims ('There is no tamarind tree. There was no innocent slave . . . There is nothing but man . . .'), and their reunion in Canada is to be understood in his terms ('To live, because afterward there is nothing . . .'). By this stage, Judith, too, seems to acquiesce in this belief. The search for transcendent meaning in such a world is clearly doomed.

The film's pessimism seems linked to what it presents as misguided attempts to take the world's surfaces as the expressions or manifestations of human desire. It is, above all, the efficacy of human agency which the film most thoroughly disavows. I argued towards the end of Chapter Two that, in melodramatic films, women often have less opportunity than men for their darker desires to issue in action, with imagination taking the place of agency (as when Lou Avery pauses in the doorway of her bedroom, in *Bigger than Life*, and 'thinks' her husband dead). Judith's recurring mental image of her husband dying in a horrific car crash certainly can be seen in such a way. The image, like so much else in *The Tamarind Seed*, is initially misleading – Judith seems to be trying to get over her husband's death, though we later discover that he died several years ago and that she had stopped loving him even earlier – and it continues to resist the sort of retrospective elucidation a Lang film might provide. However, it is still suggestive that, after the credits, the two appearances of the car crash image occur, first, when Judith has just left her unpleasant lover, Richard, thoroughly disillusioned with his false promises and insincerity, and, second, when she has gone to bed with Feodor for the first time, after earlier declaring herself to be 'very determined not to make the same mistake twice' (her reluctance also suggested, perhaps, when he'd first told her of the plan to return to Barbados, and she replied 'I'm suddenly very cold'). So the burning car of her imaginings – whose fiery explosions are mirrored by the bomb in Barbados which apparently kills Feodor – can be taken to be something like a wish to be rid of the various men in her life, which, in reality, only leads to an injury to herself. In this sense, then, Judith's motives may be more accessible to us than Feodor's, but they are certainly not obvious, especially to Feodor, despite his claim that he 'can see straight through you like glass', when he attributes motives of kindness and discretion to Judith for the censored version she gives him of Loder's unkind remarks about Feodor's bad intentions. (Ed Avery in *Bigger than Life*, on the other hand, is more accurate when he tells his wife Lou, 'I see through you as clearly as I see through this glass pitcher,' since his apparent paranoia about her antagonism towards him is, at some level, accurate enough.)

However, the fact remains that the acting out of Judith's wishes is blocked. In fact, the motives of virtually everyone in *The Tamarind Seed* are either enigmatic and unknown or ineffective. Thus, Feodor, who earlier told Judith he would never defect to the West because of his love for his country, ends up doing precisely that because of circumstances beyond his control. Judith, who has resisted going to bed with him, ends up doing so to save his life (by preventing him from going swimming in full view of potential assassins). Fergus Stephenson has no choice but to continue to betray his country to the Russians, though he has long ago become disillusioned with his Communist ideals. And Margaret Stephenson must live with a husband whom she bitterly hates (as she puts it, 'I'd enjoy seeing you hang. But I'm tied to you').

If *Beyond a Reasonable Doubt* is an example of 'massively suppressive narrative', as Pye suggests, then *The Tamarind Seed* may best be described as massively repressive, in that desire and agency are separated to an extraordinary extent. The surfaces which characters and events present to the world appear inert and unanimated by motivating desires. One may speculate about the meaning of what is seen and heard (the characters do so frequently, from Loder and his men wondering what various bits of information mean, to Judith and Feodor debating the significance of the tamarind seeds, but the world's appearances continue to resist interpretation, at least as an accurate indicator and reflection of human motivation and agency. Even Golitsyn and Loder seem to be caught up, at times, in an almost mechanical fulfilment of their duty. Thus, Golitsyn tells one of his men, with what seems almost like regret, that he is 'only following instructions' in having Feodor watched. If desire is not dead in such a world, its efficacy is certainly curtailed.

Central to the film's project are the resemblances not just between Russian and British espionage generally, but between Feodor and Fergus in particular. Just as General Golitsyn is the Russian version of Loder (the film insists on a number of close parallels between them), so Feodor is intimately linked with Fergus in an even tighter constellation of shared traits (though, whereas Feodor is outranked by Golitsyn, Fergus clearly outranks Loder, whom we observe reporting to Fergus in the latter's office and calling him 'sir'). In place of Judith's assumption that Marxism 'is based on righting a basic wrong, some people with far too much, others with nothing', Feodor can see only the corrupted face of Communism, claiming, 'I don't feel anything for the socialist revolution anymore'. On the other hand, when Fergus's wife discovers he's a traitor, he defends Marxism to her: 'It's not filth. You wouldn't understand it. You wouldn't know an ideal if you saw one . . . an ideology, for the betterment of humanity. I believed in it for a long time.' And yet his use of the past tense (like Feodor's use of the word 'anymore') suggests that he too has become disillusioned with an earlier ideal and is just as disgusted with the dirty tricks used by both sides to achieve their ends, answering Loder's curiosity over how long it will take Feodor to try to 'pull Judith in' with disapproval: 'It's *dirty*. You know, I can't help feeling *sorry* for her.' Although he is here playing the part of the loyal British diplomat, his words have the ring of truth, especially as it is not what his British colleague would like to hear.

Both Fergus and Feodor betray their countries, switching their allegiance from the British to the Russians, in the former case, and from the Russians to the British in the latter, and both men have marriages in name only: Feodor, because he is estranged from his wife by the intensity of her commitment to the socialist revolution, Fergus because of his homosexuality and Margaret's consequent withdrawal and sense of personal betrayal. Neither wife is willing to accept departures from strict ideological or sexual norms, and both women are decisive when their husbands' political subversiveness becomes known to them (though, in the case of Feodor's wife, Elena Maximova, we only know this via hearsay, as she never appears on screen). In both cases, too, any cracks in the appearance of a happy marriage or of commitment to one's country may lead to ruin and even cause Feodor's and Fergus's deaths: we need merely compare Feodor's comment on why he wants to prevent his wife from divorcing him – 'I like to stay alive' – with Fergus opening a drawer containing a gun, clearly on the brink of an expeditious suicide, after he discovers that Margaret knows he's a Communist spy, but before she reveals her self-interested plan to keep it quiet.

The film implies – through Golitsyn's comment to Feodor about a rumour to this effect – that Feodor himself is the person who originally recruited Blue (the Russians' code name for Fergus) to the Soviet side, though Feodor remarks that he doesn't even know who Blue is: 'Nobody knows that except Panyushkin'. Given the secrecy surrounding the identity of Blue, it is plausible that Feodor should have been the one who recruited him. Otherwise, it is difficult to explain how Feodor could have identified him to Loder when he defected. Although we assume that when we see Feodor stealing papers from a file, it is the Blue file, it seems too easy for him – and indeed for many other people in the organisation – to get access to it if it really does contain information about Blue's identity. Indeed, the suspense generated by his theft of the documents is somewhat gratuitous, as it's made clear that Feodor has the authority simply to have signed out the documents. So it makes sense that Feodor and Fergus are linked as recruiter and recruitee, and Feodor's naming him to Loder as the price of his own defection provides a symmetrical undoing of this past act.

However, if Fergus is a reflection of Feodor, or of the 'bad' part of Feodor which he wishes to disown – the part of him, that is, which is entangled in a corrupt world of personal and public betrayals once justified by an appeal to a youthful idealism but now hopelessly out of touch with the realities of modern ideological warfare – Feodor can extricate himself only by becoming the very thing he seeks to disown: a traitor. Although his motive is self-preservation, it is still an essentially self-defeating act, and he is symbolically 'killed' when, during the stopover with Judith in Barbados (from where he will continue on to Canada to go into hiding without her), his holiday villa is bombed by Golitsyn's men and Judith is burned in the process. As far as Judith, Fergus, and the Russians are aware, Feodor is now dead. At the same time, Fergus, thinking Feodor's death has put him out of danger, is unaware of the precariousness of his own position: he is being allowed to continue to pass on information to the Russians which is now carefully monitored by the British and of little value, hastening the day when the Russians will finally conclude that he's a double agent and dispose of him themselves. Yet his actions, too, seem to have been self-destructive, not only in the haste with which he turned to suicide as a solution to his problems only barely averted by Margaret's entrance into the room, but, equally, in the way he left his incriminating cigarette lighter at home, where Margaret could easily find it. If this is indeed an instance of Freudian inadvertence, then (unconsciously, at

The Tamarind Seed.
The injured Judith
(Julie Andrews) recoils
from Loder.

least) Fergus – like Feodor – also seems to want to escape from the vicious circles in which he moves, even if it means dying.

All of the film's main male characters – Fergus with his lighter, Golitsyn with his cigarette holder, Feodor with his Russian cigarettes, Loder with his pipes and cigar, MacLeod smoking in bed – are men who smoke like chimneys, Dimitri standing in for them all in Sandy Mitchell's comment that he 'smokes like a *truba*'. When Loder goes to visit Judith at the convalescent home in Barbados where she's recovering from her burns, and he casually lights his pipe, Judith (who had refused Feodor's offer of a Russian cigarette when they first met, telling him she doesn't smoke) reacts fearfully, reminded of the fire which had caused her injuries. She also, perhaps, at a more symbolic level, is reacting to Loder himself (as she does when she pulls back from him earlier in the scene) and all that he represents, not least the inability to keep her and Feodor safe. (Of course, although Judith and the film's viewers don't know it yet, Feodor is, in fact, alive, but, as we've seen, this is due to the merest chance; in any case, when Feodor was pulled out of the bungalow before the blast, Judith was left inside, and the indifference to her fate displayed by this act was considerably worse in terms of its callous disregard for whether she lived or died than mere incompetence would have been.) Judith, Margaret and Rachel – the fragile wife of Judith's former lover – are casualties of the world of political intrigue occupied by their men, all of whose marriages are in considerable disarray (as was Judith's in the past). Judith's present injuries confirm the symbolism of the poisonous tree about which Feodor had warned her when they met; rain falling through its branches onto those taking shelter beneath 'will burn your skin' if she ignores his warning.

Margaret recognises her affinities with Rachel, in this respect, when she takes her under her wing with what appears to be sincere concern ('She needs someone to stand up for her. He's such a cold-blooded swine. I wish I'd had someone to stand up for *me*'). Yet in spite of the male victimisation of women in these relationships, the film extends a degree of sympathy to some of the men as well, and above all to Fergus

The Tamarind Seed. An image of entrapment: Judith and Feodor (Omar Sharif) behind railings.

for whom, as a homosexual, marriage is especially oppressive. His prominent position and society's prevailing attitudes to homosexuality prevent his having ready recourse to blatant extramarital affairs, in contrast to both Feodor and Richard, whose heterosexual philanderings are tacitly condoned and even encouraged as long as they are politically useful and pose no risk to security. That Margaret is herself having an affair with MacLeod – which she flaunts to her husband's face without identifying her lover – only adds to the poignancy of his situation. Both his concern for the children when he thinks his political treachery is about to be revealed, and a comment he makes to Richard – 'I had a couple of postings myself when Margaret couldn't join me, and I remember I got very lonely' – seem genuine and oddly touching. Although some of the characters are clearly more sympathetic than others, they are all, to varying degrees, simultaneously complicit with, and the product of, circumstances beyond their knowledge and full control, and details of the film's visual imagery bear this out, even for those characters with considerable power. In fact, the pervasive images of entrapment are the least opaque in the film, perhaps because their undermining of our sense of the characters' freedom (an undermining of what I earlier referred to as the efficacy of their desires) is precisely their point. For example, when Loder meets Judith at the zoo to plan the final details of Feodor's defection, he and Judith are first seen on the far side of the tiger's cage, revealed as if behind bars once the tiger, which was blocking our view of them, has moved offscreen to the left. This scene follows Feodor's removal of papers from the Blue file, where both Feodor's tie and the dress of the Russian woman official who fetches the file are striped like the tiger who, despite his powerful appearance, is still a prisoner in the cage, and we see Feodor leave by the lift whose metalwork frame is also cage-like. No one is exempt, not even Golitsyn, who is subject to the same imagery and implications when he enters the lift in another scene.

The sense we get of people reacting to circumstances over which they have little control renders ambiguous any simple attributions of guilt or innocence, which would

The Tamarind Seed.
Judith, Loder
(Anthony Quayle) and
the tiger.

presuppose a context of informed freedom of choice. Although Judith tells Feodor, 'I very much believe in being free to choose', her belief in 'innocent slaves and miraculous tamarind seeds', if taken as a broader statement about human powerless-ness and divine justice, seems to contradict this. Her belief in what Feodor refers to as 'fairy-tales' is not, in fact, so different from his belief in fate: 'That way, if any-thing goes wrong, it is never our fault, it is fate.' However, although this implies a shared conviction that human behaviour is subordinate to larger forces – producing an innocence of sorts, though as the result of external control rather than conscious choice – the force in which Judith believes is a just one, whereas Feodor's 'fate' is indifferent to good and evil alike. Thus, his intention is merely 'To live, because afterward there is nothing, no reward for the good, no punishment for the evil.'

That the corrupt world will carry on as before is made clear when Loder leaves the convalescent home with MacLeod in a car and instructs him as follows, though to no obvious purpose: 'Oh, by the way, when we get back I want you to call Mrs Stephenson. Start seeing her again. Find out if she knows that her husband's a . . . a Russian agent.' The conversation is counterpointed with a shot of Fergus looking happy and relaxed at the dining-room table with his wife and children, ignorant of the fate hanging over him. For Judith and Feodor, too, their future happiness is by no means assured, despite Feodor's insistence on withdrawing from the world of political intrigue after the delivery of the Blue file. For one thing, Judith's track record with men does not inspire confidence, and her comment about her husband ('If he hadn't been killed, I would have left him'), as well as the break-up with Richard, suggests her tendency to make a quick exit when relationships go stale. Feodor's reply – 'Well, you won't be allowed to leave me' – as well as his comment when insisting on his wish to go for a swim in Barbados, against Loder's orders – 'When I'm in Canada, Mr Loder can treat me like a prisoner, but not before' – surround their future prospects with images of coercion and entrapment. Further, Loder's previous failure to keep them safe undercuts any remaining optimism we may feel.

The Tamarind Seed. Final dissolve as the couple move away and the credits being to roll.

The intelligence and pessimism of the film, as well as the intricate interpenetration of its sexual relationships with political intrigue, and the questioning of easy ascriptions of innocence and guilt, are reminiscent of Alfred Hitchcock's political thrillers. When Fergus's wife Margaret visits her lover MacLeod in an early scene, the fact that, when Margaret arrives, MacLeod is watching a Hitchcock spy thriller – *Foreign Correspondent* (1940) – makes the connections explicit. The first of the two telescoped parts of the Hitchcock film that we see shows the assassination of the pacifist Van Meer (Albert Basserman). However, the murdered man turns out to be a double for Van Meer so that his allies will assume he is dead and the *real* Van Meer can be tortured for the details of a secret treaty. The second clip shows Johnny Jones (Joel McCrea), an 'innocent' American journalist, who discovers that Van Meer is still alive and gets caught up in an effort to discover his whereabouts. As he hides in a windmill to spy on the villains, the sleeve of his overcoat gets caught up in the powerful mechanism of the mill. Van Meer's bogus death – and the equally unpleasant fate which awaits him alive – as well as the image of the coat sleeve of the naive reporter in the remorseless grip of the windmill's mechanism have obvious, though hardly cheering, relevance to *The Tamarind Seed*.

Feodor, too, has undergone a symbolic death only to re-emerge in another part of the same repressive world, although this time he takes Judith with him as they walk away from the camera into the depths of the screen. The dissolve at this point has the effect of suddenly relocating them much further away, producing an uncanny feeling of sudden diminishment and irretrievable distance, while also recalling the dreamy dissolves in the early moments of the film, thus emphasising even further the illusory and precarious nature of Judith's and Feodor's relationship in the film's final shots, while Loder's cumbersome machinery continues to turn.

MEN AND ROMANCE

The working hypothesis in this chapter has been that the terms governing the representation of the romantic couple in American films are crucially dependent upon whether they are located within a melodramatic or a comedic narrative world. In trying to establish what the melodramatic world is like, the films that were considered in Chapter Two were deliberately chosen to avoid the complicating issue of romance, though heterosexual relationships are still central to their structures and concerns in the pervasiveness with which desire is shown to be repressed, displaced and subjected to vigorous symbolic attack. The present chapter has examined what happens when heterosexual desire is both active and openly acknowledged within melodramatic films, but with the same repressive and destructive energies poised to submit it to the same aggressive denials as when it is either inactive (as with Ed and Lou in *Bigger than Life*) or covert (as with Goeth's desire for Helen Hirsch in *Schindler's List*). To what extent can it be seen positively and survive such attacks?

Our understanding of the melodramatic world needs to be modified where romance is introduced. In Chapter Two, I posited a fantasy 'elsewhere' in which the male's struggles with heterosexual desire (in cases where it is forbidden or represents a threat of diminishment within the domestic sphere) can be played out in a more displaced fashion. This contrast between 'here' (the ordinary social world) and 'elsewhere' (the space of male fantasy where displaced battles against heterosexual desire can take place) splits the melodramatic world into two separate domains, and the differences between them are fairly clear-cut. This is not to say that we can point with any confidence to a precise physical boundary where one ends and the other begins (for example, where the small town becomes the city, or where civilisation turns into the wilderness, or where the home front turns into the battlefield); on the contrary, the two domains are rarely shown in the same scene, let alone the same shot. The Western hero can't be said to be in the wilderness until the homestead or small community is well and truly out of sight, nor is the soldier back home until the battlefield is far away. There is a certain no-man's land between them. Even Scott's fall into the basement in *The Incredible Shrinking Man* suggests, through his state of unconsciousness, that the two spaces, though adjacent, exist on discrete symbolic planes, and the ordinary world upstairs might just as well be a million miles away for all its accessibility to Scott from that point on. So the 'here' and the 'elsewhere' of melodramatic films have an intervening space between them, in contrast to the way that the space of romance tends to be embedded fully within the surrounding social world. It should also be noted that what functions as 'elsewhere' in one film can function as 'here' in another: thus, the city is a very different place in the context of a typical *film noir* and in a sophisticated comedy of remarriage. Similarly, the meaning of the wide-open spaces beyond the frontier may be reversed in those Westerns which see the Indians, rather than the Whites, as representing the values of community and home.

Romance introduces a third significant space, the shared domain (psychological as well as physical) of the romantic couple, which is usually carved out as a private area within the social world, rather than beyond its boundaries. Because of this close proximity to the larger social world, the repressiveness of that world is close at hand within melodramatic films, and the melodramatic romantic relationship can be seen as continually under siege, in contrast to the freedoms inherent in the 'elsewhere' of male fantasy, where one often has a much greater sense of energies bursting forth from conventional restraints, if generally in the form of violence rather than erotic release. Thus, for the couples at the end of both *An Affair to Remember* and *The Tamarind Seed*, there is a powerful feeling of contraction of possibilities and of withdrawal from the larger world, with the private romantic space now becoming a sort of prison or symbolic death. The earlier erotic sparks which energised these couples have been all but extinguished by the circumstances of the melodramatic plots (Terry's accident, which has immobilised her in a wheelchair, and Judith's injuries from the explosion in the bungalow, which have left her drained of energy and deathly pale). For both women, it has proved dangerous to have chosen to be with these men, though it is also true that they have resisted them at various points (indeed, I suggested earlier that Terry's accident itself might be seen as a kind of symbolic resistance): the combinations of danger and resistance are clear indications that we are in the presence of romantic melodrama.

Among comedic films, it is more difficult to come up with examples that exclude romance, because the strategy of repressing heterosexual desire within the social world and converting it into an aggressive assertion of difference 'elsewhere' is not available, nor is it necessary, since in a comedic context sexual desire tends to be more openly acknowledged without guilt and without it being perceived as a threat. Romance within a comedic context, as discussed in Chapter Three, provides a useful contrast with the films in the present chapter, which are either romantic melodramas or – in the case of *The Courtship of Eddie's Father* – a romance which hovers between the melodramatic and the comedic. This hesitation between the two is not as atypical as may at first appear. I've suggested that romance posits a private space embedded within the social world. If melodramatic films present the social world as essentially repressive and rejecting of the romantic couple's expressions of mutual erotic desire (except in terms of a narrowly defined, constricted hierarchical model), with their private space under siege from the world outside, comedic films, by contrast, allow the positive eroticism of the romantic couple and the safety of the larger world – or at least the immediate community, however that is defined – to coexist in a state of mutual hospitality.

One consequence of such proximity between the private romantic space and the public social one in melodramatic and comedic films alike is that the same structure can yield up romances of either type, thus allowing for transformations from one to the other in the course of a single film. We've already seen how, in *The Courtship of Eddie's Father*, Tom carves out a private space within which to develop a positive emotional relationship with his son (their relationship not precisely a romantic one, of course, but an interesting variant upon it), which has the power to open up a larger shared space at the end of the film capable of including Elizabeth as well, just as it has already expanded, largely through the use of comedy, to incorporate Dollye and Jerry (beginning with Dollye when she is included in Tom and Eddie's night out, which had started as a movie and dinner for just the two of them and turned into a shared date for all three). On the other hand, Elizabeth's earlier invasions of Tom's and Eddie's space were more repressive in that they excluded Tom from his new-found emotional closeness to Eddie. To the extent that romance can be seen to liberate the couple, at least privately, from the rigid, gender-based roles and inequalities which prevail in the larger world outside – and thus to be a threat to its hierarchical structures – melodrama's assault on the boundaries of the private world, from the outside in, tends to transform such liberation into fantasies of diminishment and augmentation, thus reconstituting the couple in melodrama's own terms, as the site of antagonistic battles for power. Comedy's strategy, on the other hand, is to link the breakdown in hierarchical structures within the romantic relationship itself (whereby the man comes to identify more positively with a female position and role, say) to a larger comic disruption in the world outside, weakening the boundaries between the private and the public, whether from the inside out, in a transformation of the surrounding social world, or from the outside in, guaranteeing the safety of the romantic relationship by its location within the sheltering safety of the world outside.

The genre of the musical produces particularly good examples of such to-and-fro struggles across the boundary between couple and community, for two related reasons. First, the image of the musicalised male tends to come across as an image of a 'softened' or 'emotionalised' male right from the start, despite attempts which may be made, through athletic choreography and robust delivery of the songs, to counteract this effect. The expressiveness of music – and the spectacle of its performance – immediately place the male in a position at odds with traditional images of stoic, emotionally self-sufficient masculinity (as does romance as well, of course). So romance in the musical reinforces an already existent utopian potential to transform the social domain. Second, however, the structural alternation, within the musical genre, between the numbers and the narrative allows the latter to suppress this potential and repair the deficits created by the former, restoring a more traditional masculinity if required. Thus, the feminisation of the male through music does not necessarily foreclose the possibility of musicals where the melodramatic reasserts itself in the end, even if the odds are against it because of the positive energies associated with the couple through music. The dichotomy between the private romantic space and the public social domain which I've described as central to romance may, in some cases, be mapped onto the dichotomy between numbers and narrative which structures the musical, so that the music which feminises the male within a private space is in conflict with the requirements of a more conventional narrative and, simultaneously, of a more repressive social world, allowing the outcome of the struggle to go either way (the community and the couple musicalised in a mutually reinforcing dynamic or the musical couple defeated and silenced by the melodramatic world outside).

A good example of this process is to be found in *The Sound of Music*. Superficially, *The Sound of Music* seems to bear a resemblance to *The Courtship of Eddie's Father* in its desire to soften the widower, Captain Von Trapp (Christopher Plummer), by making him emotionally open and responsive to his children, in this case through music, and the scenes where this happens do succeed and give pleasure up to a point. However, whereas Tom specifically takes the place of Eddie's dead mother in Minnelli's film (with Elizabeth's desire to take on that role perceived as a threat, as we've seen), Captain Von Trapp never deviates from a very traditional paternal role, and exhibits none of Tom Corbett's turmoil or emotional depth, nor does either the Captain or the film find the prospect of Maria (Julie Andrews) taking his dead wife's place a problem. Quite the contrary. Containing her energies within such a traditional female role is indeed the solution to the problem Maria has presented in the early moments of the film (for example, in the song, 'How Do You Solve a Problem Like Maria?'). The film gives the Captain a song or two to soften his military bearing and bring some warmth to his repressive façade – presumably to prevent our confusing him with the Nazis in the larger melodramatic world outside his home – but the transformation is superficial and short-lived. Not only does the Nazi world increasingly threaten the private space of his family and marriage, but he himself is disturbingly linked to the Nazis in ways that the film never openly faces up to, let alone subjects to critical scrutiny. Even in the scene of his so-called transformation, the song he chooses to sing – 'Edelweiss' – is troubling both in its nationalism and in the image of white purity which is used to symbolise his country and (through his gaze at Maria while he sings) his future wife. It is difficult not to be aware of this imagery in the context of a film about Nazis, even one in which Aryan purity is never mentioned, and the so-called 'Jewish Problem' and the Germans' 'Final Solution' are replaced by the 'solution' to the 'problem' of Maria. The language of 'whiteness', 'purity', 'problems' and 'solutions' persists, however, and hopelessly muddles the film's project to soften the Captain and marry him off to Maria.

In his article on *The Sound of Music* in *Movie* No. 23 (Winter 1976/77), Richard Dyer points out how the music disappears from the film in the final stages of the narrative. The replacement of musical numbers by narrative developments is paralleled, as I've already suggested, by a move from a comedic narrative world to a more melodramatic one centred upon the struggle of the couple (and their family) against the repressive Nazi world of occupied Austria. The film might have concluded in a number of ways: Nazis transformed by musical family (an unlikely outcome, given historical realities, though the performance by the Von Trapps at the Salzburg Festival provokes a mild expression of anti-Nazi feeling from the audience who join in their patriotic song); family defeated by repressive regime (too abrupt a reversal for the film to sustain by this point); or stalemate (with the family escaping to an alternative 'private space' abroad, while the Nazi regime continues to flourish back home). The film avoids either the first (comedic) or the second (melodramatic) outcome, but tries to give us a positive representation of their escape while unable to suppress fully our knowledge, as historically informed viewers, of the Nazi atrocities that lie ahead. However, the romantic relationship of Captain Von Trapp and Maria – despite moments of charm and humour, however self-conscious, in Christopher Plummer's performance, as well as the initial energy and exuberance in that of Julie Andrews, and even the hints of romantic comedy in the initial sparring between them – is ultimately unconvincing. Once married, Maria is significantly diminished in both rebelliousness and the playful energies which linked her with the children earlier on, now deferring to her husband's will and decisions and sublimating her interests in favour of his. In his confrontation with the young Nazi who is on the point of preventing their escape by blowing the whistle on them as they emerge from their hiding-places, the Captain is once again emotionally cold: 'You'll never be one of them.' His words make clear his attitude to the boy's softness and weakness – to his inability to be much of a man – and the Captain's contempt for him on that account. So the capacity of romance, or music, to transform the world is blocked not simply by the repressiveness of the world outside, but by the couple's internalisation of such ideological norms, especially where male and female roles are concerned, and the comedic skills of the two actors are ultimately defeated by the requirements of a repressive script.

Despite the distinction between the 'elsewhere' of male fantasy and the socially embedded private space of the romantic couple, it is clear that the romantic space is also a product of fantasy, though of a radically different kind. In place of the violent assertions of one's difference from others, romance provides a fantasy of mutual identification and reciprocal desire. It too may represent a space to which the be-leaguered male can flee when the demands of a repressive world – and of being a man within it – become too great. This idea of romance as a haven or escape is central to another musical, *Brigadoon* (1954, directed by Vincente Minnelli). In this film, the romantic couple – Tommy Albright and Fiona Campbell – and the surrounding com-munity of Brigadoon, into which Tommy and his friend Jeff Douglas wander while on a hunting trip in Scotland, are, from the start, not easily separable: the couple and the village are part of a single magical space. Thus, Fiona's first words to Tommy ('You're in Brigadoon') are spoken as he turns and sees her for the first time, and Tommy himself conflates Fiona with Brigadoon when he explains to Jeff why he's decided to stay ('Jeff, I tell you I feel more a part of her and all this than I . . . than I ever felt about Jane or anybody or anything back home'). His desire to stay with Fiona is inseparable from his feeling that he belongs in this place. In any case, because of the 'miracle' which isolates the town from the world by having one hundred years go by in the outside world for each night that passes in Brigadoon, a miracle which puts the entire village at risk if anyone who belongs there should leave, Tommy's desire to stay with Fiona is actually a decision to remain in Brigadoon forever. So, although most romances mark out a private space within the larger social one, Brigadoon manages to integrate the couple fully within a utopian community while, at the same time, imposing insurmountable boundaries between the world of Brigadoon and the larger world beyond, as represented, in particular, by New York City. Tommy is transformed by Brigadoon – and by Fiona as its embodiment; their romance, however, does not in any way transform Brigadoon, and Brigadoon itself is powerless to change New York and the negative qualities it represents. Rather than risk the corruption of the village by leaving it open to siege from threatening influences originating outside, the late Mr Forsythe, in his prayers, had arranged for its isolation. Brigadoon can neither be corrupted by that world nor transform it in turn.

But one man's blessing is another man's curse, and Harry Beaton, who loves Fiona's sister Jean (Virginia Bosler) but has lost her to Charlie Dalrymple (Jimmy Thompson), sees Brigadoon not as a miraculous place of reciprocated desire, but as 'this cursed town', as, in fact, it must appear to those whose desires are blocked and frustrated within it. One can compare this to Feodor's comment to Judith, in *The Tamarind Seed*, when she refuses him her bed: 'If this is what I have to expect if I come over to the West, then I am better off dead.' And Harry is indeed accidentally shot and killed by the cynical, hard-drinking Jeff – Harry's counterpart from the world outside – when Harry attempts to escape from Brigadoon, a place that has no positive connotation for either man. When Jeff and Tommy leave the confines of the village for home, and Brigadoon disappears in the mist, New York emerges from it, implying that New York is a fantasy world as well, the negative mirror image of Brigadoon. That Jeff is Harry's equivalent is suggested by Jeff's own drunken words to the bartender back home, who questions him when he mentions Brigadoon: 'That was the name of my brother who ran away.' That Tommy and Charlie Dalrymple end up as 'brothers' too – given their respective marriages to sisters – is just as clear. In fact, this is evident from an even earlier stage, in the number 'I'll Go Home with Bonnie Jean', which functions to integrate Tommy – and, to an extent, Jeff as well –

into the community through song and dance, and links Tommy and Charlie by their shared ability to reach the high notes of the song, much of the humour of the number centred upon this friendly competition, which proves to be a much greater strain for Jeff, thus confirming Brigadoon as a place where feminised men seem most at home. Tommy's ultimate return to Brigadoon and to Fiona is a foregone conclusion. Without romance, the private space and, in this film at least, the community as its natural extension, risk becoming intolerable. It is evident from this example that whether a given film is melodramatic or comedic is related in some way to issues concerning point of view, as we have seen before. *Brigadoon*, if constructed more consistently from Jeff's or Harry's point of view, rather than from Tommy's, would be a much more melodramatic film.

The prevailing moods and structures of melodramatic and comedic films give rise to very different treatments of romance and other matters of shared concern, such as what it means to be a man, and whether love and freedom can go hand in hand. The fantasies of characters within these films – that is, the ways of imagining such matters which are available to them – may overlap with those offered to us, or they may be quite distinct. We know that we are watching a film, and the possible fantasies and trains of thought open to us are much less restricted than those of any one character who is forced to take the world's appearances more literally and to observe them from a more limited point of view. The most interesting American films derive much of their richness and depth from complex and subtly textured narrative worlds and rhetorical strategies – as we have seen in those under examination here – and display an intricate interplay between melodramatic and comedic moments and spaces, and between characters placed centre-stage and those on the margins.

REFERENCES

Works cited in the text appear, on the first occasion, with full details, as below. Thereafter, the reference is abbreviated to the surname of the author (e.g. Gledhill, p.106), with a date if more than one publication by the same author is referred to in the course of the book (e.g. Wood 1979, p.96).

Andrew Britton, *Cary Grant: Comedy and Male Desire*, Tyneside Cinema, Newcastle-upon-Tyne, 1983

Bill Bryson, *Made in America*, Secker & Warburg, London, 1994

Ian Cameron (ed.), *The Movie Book of Film Noir*, Studio Vista, London, 1992

Ian Cameron & Douglas Pye (eds), *The Movie Book of the Western*, Studio Vista, London, 1996

Stanley Cavell, *Pursuits of Happiness: The Hollywood Comedy of Remarriage*, Harvard University Press, Cambridge, Massachusetts, 1981

Richard Dyer, 'The Sound of Music,' *Movie* no. 23, London, 1976-77

Wes D. Gehring, *Screwball Comedy: A Genre of Madcap Romance*, Greenwood Press, Westport, Connecticut, 1986

Christine Gledhill (ed.), *Home Is Where the Heart Is: Studies in Melodrama and the Woman's Film*, British Film Institute, London, 1987

Terry Lovell, *Pictures of Reality: Aesthetics, Politics and Pleasure*, British Film Institute, London, 1980

Andrew Horton (ed.), *Comedy/Cinema/Theory*, University of California Press, Berkeley, California, 1991

Kristine Brunovska Karnick/Henry Jenkins (eds), *Classical Hollywood Comedy*, Routledge, London, 1995

Richard Maltby/Ian Craven, *Hollywood Cinema: An Introduction*, Blackwell Publishers, Oxford, 1995

Gerald Mast, *The Comic Mind: Comedy and the Movies*, New English Library, London, 1973

Steve Neale & Frank Krutnik, *Popular Film and Television Comedy*, Routledge, London, 1990

V.F. Perkins, 'Comedies,' *Movie* no. 5, London, 1962

V.F. Perkins, *Film as Film: Understanding and Judging Movies*, Penguin, London 1972

Douglas Pye, 'Genre and Movies,' *Movie* no. 20, London, 1975

Tzvetan Todorov, *The Fantastic: A Structural Approach to a Literary Genre*, Cornell University Press, Ithaca, New York, 1975

George M. Wilson, *Narration in Light: Studies in Cinematic Point of View*, Johns Hopkins University Press, Baltimore, Maryland, 1986

Michael Wood, *America in the Movies*, Secker & Warburg, London, 1975

Robin Wood, 'The American Family Comedy: from *Meet Me In St. Louis* to *The Texas Chainsaw Massacre*,' *Wide Angle* vol. 3, no. 2, Johns Hopkins University Press, Baltimore, Maryland, 1979

Robin Wood, *Howard Hawks*, revised edition, British Film Institute, London, 1981

INDEX OF FILMS